Famous Battles of the Early Modern Period

Chris McNab

New York

Cataloging-in-Publication Data

Names: McNab, Chris.
Title: Famous battles of the early modern period / Chris McNab.
Description: New York : Cavendish Square Publishing, 2018. | Series: Classic warfare | Includes bibliographical references and index.
Identifiers: ISBN 9781502632500 (library bound)
Subjects: LCSH: Battles--Juvenile literature. | Military history--Juvenile literature.

Classification: LCC D25.M37 2018 | DDC 355.4/8--dc23

Editorial Director: David McNamara
Editor: Michael Sciandra
Associate Art Director: Amy Greenan
Production Coordinator: Karol Szymczuk

Printed in the United States of America

The photographs in this book are used by permission and through the courtesy of: AKG Images: 7 bottom (Peter Connolly), 16 (Erich Lessing), 30–31 (Maximilianeum Collection), 36 (Peter Connolly), 64–65, 72 (Coll. Archiv F. Kunst & Geschichte), 74 (Cameraphoto), 81 (Coll. Archiv F. Kunst & Geschichte), 86–87, 89 (Westfaelisches Schulmuseum), 90–91 (Bibliotheque Nationale), 108 (World History Archive), 111 (Bibliotheque Nationale), 126 (Cameraphoto), 128–129 (Cameraphoto), 140 (Coll. Archiv F. Kunst & Geschichte), 156 (British Library), 168 (Coll. Archiv F. Kunst & Geschichte), 172–173 (Erich Lessing), 179 (Visioars), 180–181 (Jerome da Cunha), 196–197 (Erich Lessing), 198 (IAM), 244 (Coll. Archiv F. Kunst & Geschichte), 270; Alamy: 48–49 (North Wind Picture Archives), 52 (Art Directors & TRIP), 104 (North Wind Picture Archives), 118 (Art Archive), 132 (Classic Images), 154 (Timewatch Images), 164–165 (Art Archive), 178 (Classic Image), 222 (Art Gallery Collection), 272–273 (Art Archive), 278–279 (Art Archive), 300–301 (Art Archive); Amber Books: 6, 7 top; Art Archive: 120–121 (National Museum Damascus/Gianni Dagli Orti), 146–147 (Pharonic Village, Cairo/Gianni Dagli Orti), 264–265 (Musée du Château de Versailles/Gianni Dagli Orti); Art-Tech/MARS: 276, 288, 295, 312; Bibliotheque Nationale de France: 102; Bridgeman Art Library: 18–19 (Look & Learn), 26, 38–39 (Giraudon), 40 (Alinari), 56 (Anne van Biema Collection), 117 (Giraudon), 170 (Agra Art), 182 (Archives Charmet), 202 (Giraudon), 208–209 (Society of Apothecaries), 227 (Maidstone Museum & Art Gallery), 234–235 (National Army Museum), 238 (Pushkin Museum), 240–241, 250–251, 254–255 (Stapleton Collection), 282 (Galleria d'Arte Moderna), 286–287 (Mansell Collection), 292–293 (Stapleton Collection), 296 & 297 (National Army Museum), 306, 308–309 (State Central Artillery Museum), 311 (National Army Museum); Corbis: 8–9 (Historical Picture Archive), 10 (Richard T. Nowitz), 13 (Jose Fuste Raga), 14 (Sandro Vannini), 44 (Bettmann), 50 (Araldo de Luca), 76 (Richard T. Nowitz), 96–97 (Stefano Bianchetti), 142 (Bettmann), 188–189 (Art Archive/Alfredo Dagli Orti), 200 (Araldo de Luca), 204 (Asian Art Archaeology), 210 (Reuters/Kim Kyung-Hoon), 216 (Werner Forman); De Agostini: 42; Mary Evans Picture Library: 28 (Edwin Mullan Collection), 34, 63, 68, 82, 122, 138, 163, 174, 220, 232, 236; Getty Images: 20 (Superstock), 54 (Hulton Archive), 98 (Hulton Archive); Library of Congress: 256, 257, 258, 304; Malta Tourist Authority: 152; Photos.com: 92, 100, 160, 206, 230, 262, 278; Photo12.com: 41 (Oronoz), 136–137 (Anne Ronan Picture Library), 158–159 (Bibliotheque Nationale), 162 (Hachette), 186 (EUK-Opid), 215 (JTB Photo); Leven Smits Creative Commons Licence: 114–115; TopFoto: 58 (Granger Collection), 246 (Ullsteinbild), 298 (RIA Novosti); Werner Forman Archive: 218–219 (Kuroada Collection); All maps © Amber Books.

CONTENTS

The Early Modern Period

Even as increasingly professional armies and the use of artillery became more widespread from the sixteenth century, many forces remained wedded to the fighting principles of an earlier age.

This was the period when bigger wasn't always better. At Breitenfeld (1631), King Gustavus Adolphus of Sweden brought off a brilliant victory over the massive but inflexible Hapsburg Imperial army, using smaller, intermingled battalions of artillery and cavalry. Too slavish an adherence to the massed cavalry charge launched into enfilading artillery fire often resulted in disaster, as at Ramillies (1706), Poltava (1708) and Minden (1757).

Kings still led armies into battle during this period—notably Gustavus Adolphus, and the brilliant Frederick the Great of Prussia at Rossbach (1757)—but increasingly it was the age of the career soldier, such as John Churchill, Duke of Marlborough, whose finest moment came at Blenheim (1704).

◀ Kahlenburg provided the Hapsburg Empire with a notable victory near Vienna over the Ottoman Turkish army, who were weakened by attempting to fight a battle on two fronts.

Brunkeberg 1471

KEY FACTS

WHO A royal army of 6000 Danish regulars and German mercenaries led by King Christian I Oldenburg of Denmark, opposed an army of 10,000 Swedish peasant levies led by Sten Sture.

WHAT Professional troops, including heavily armored knights, were defeated by lightly armed but numerous peasant troops.

WHERE Brunkeberg, west of Stockholm, Sweden.

WHEN October 10, 1471

WHY As part of a long-standing conflict, the Swedes, seeking full independence, clashed with the Danish king, seeking to restore royal (Danish) control over Sweden by seizing Stockholm.

OUTCOME The Danes overconfidently charged the Swedes, who, using superior numbers and knowledge of the local terrain, encircled and defeated their foe.

The battle of Brunkeberg not only saved the nascent Swedish nation state from being submerged in a Danish-dominated Scandinavian Union but saw a modern, professional army defeated and routed by a committed and well-organized peasant militia.

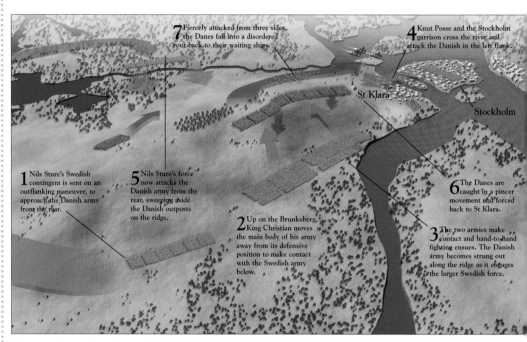

7 Fiercely attacked from three sides, the Danes fall into a disordered rout back to their waiting ships.

4 Knut Posse and the Stockholm garrison cross the river and attack the Danish in the left flank.

St Klara

Stockholm

1 Nils Sture's Swedish contingent is sent on an outflanking maneuver, to approach the Danish army from the rear.

5 Nils Sture's force now attacks the Danish army from the rear, sweeping aside the Danish outposts on the ridge.

6 The Danes are caught in a pincer movement and forced back to St Klara.

2 Up on the Brunkeberg, King Christian moves the main body of his army away from its defensive position to make contact with the Swedish army below.

3 The two armies make contact and hand-to-hand fighting ensues. The Danish army becomes strung out along the ridge as it engages the larger Swedish force.

It has never been a foregone conclusion that a powerful modern army will overcome a primitive smaller one. At Brunkeberg, superior local knowledge swung things decisively in favor of Sten Sture.

LOCATION

Brunkeberg ⊹ •Stockholm

SWEDEN

DENMARK

If Christian I had managed to capture Stockholm, at the center of the kingdom of Sweden, he would have controlled the whole north-central Baltic.

At Brunkeberg two vastly different armies met. The Danish had mounted knights and hardened professional mercenaries from Germany, who liked to fight regular battles in the open field. The core of the Swedes' army was made up of peasant levies armed with swords, pikes, axes, crossbows and longbows. The favorite tactic among the Swedish peasants was the ambush, and at Brunkeberg, Sten Sture would use that tactic to good effect.

Sture knew that on the high, wooded and boulder-strewn ridge of Brunkeberg, where the Danes had positioned themselves, knights in armor, artillery and regular infantry would not be in their element. While his army attacked the Danes from the front against the slopes leading up to their camp, Nils Sture took his fierce force of Darlecarlians around the ridge to attack the vulnerable rear of the Danish position from the east, overcoming them through a combination of surprise and sheer numbers. Here the training and superior arms of King Christian's king's troops were of little avail as wave after wave of snarling Swedes poured in on them from all sides. Christian lost half his men and Sten Sture had saved Sweden's fledgling statehood and independence.

TIMELINE

1500–1000BC	1000–500BC	500BC–0AD	0–500AD	500–1000AD	1000–1500AD	1500–6,000AD

Diu 1509

KEY FACTS

Who Dom Francisco de Almeida leads the Portugese fleet, against the joint fleet and soldiers of the Sultan of Gujarat, the Mamluk Sultanate of Egypt, and the Zamorin of Kozhikode.

What The Egyptians' land-based artillery was little match for the heavy cannon of Dom Francisco's fleet, which simply blocked the harbor and blasted them away.

Where Off the Indian coast, near Diu.

When February 3, 1509

Why The Portuguese Empire was gradually extending its control of the seas, but its ships were subject to frequent attack by the Egyptian fleet.

Outcome After victory, the Portuguese were able to consolidate by gaining control of several ports in the region, taking effective control of the Indian Ocean.

Dom Francisco de Almeida – "the Great Dom Francisco" – was a Portuguese adventurer with a great many exploits to his name. When his son was killed in a battle with Egyptian ships, he was determined, as viceroy of Portuguese India, to gain revenge at Diu.

Dom Francisco de Almeida arrived at Diu with a high reputation as a military leader, but in reality this was a vengeance mission after the Egyptians had killed his son.

LOCATION

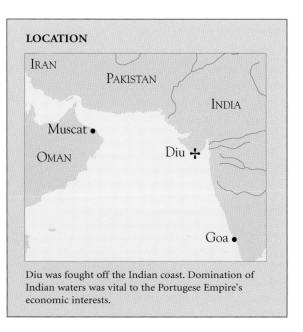

Diu was fought off the Indian coast. Domination of Indian waters was vital to the Portugese Empire's economic interests.

Establishing control of the Indian Ocean was central to Portuguese ambitions to build a naval empire, but it inevitably caused friction with other trading powers in the region. When an attack on Portuguese ships by an allied fleet led by the Mamluk Egyptians resulted in the death of the son of the Indian vicerory Dom Francisco de Almeida, retaliation was inevitable.

A pretext was not hard to find. Diu was a key port in the Indian Ocean, so Dom Francisco launched a gunship bombardment from outside the harbor. The Egyptians attempted to respond by use of artillery encamped within the city, but with little success. The small ships they attempted to launch were no more successful. They were too light to carry cannon, and for those that did manage to get close enough to engage in boarding and hand to hand combat, their sailors were outfought by well-armored Portuguese equipped with arquebuses and grenades. The result was a rollicking Portuguese victory, to further stamp their emergence as the masters of oceans.

TIMELINE

1500–1000BC	1000–500BC	500BC–0AD	0–500AD	500–1000AD	1000–1500AD	1500–2000AD

Novara 1513

KEY FACTS

WHO French general Louis de la Trémoille (1460–1525) against Milanese leader, Maximilian Sforza (1493–1530), and his mercenary Swiss soldiers.

WHAT The French army of 10,000 were besieging Novara, a Milanese city, when attacked by a relief force largely composed of Swiss mercenaries employed by the Duke of Milan.

WHERE Near Novara, northern Italy.

WHEN June 6, 1513

WHY The French had been victorious at Ravenna the previous year. Nevertheless, the French under King Louis XII were driven out of the city of Milan the following month by the Holy League.

OUTCOME The French defeat by the Swiss pikemen forced Louis XII (1462–1515) to withdraw from Milan and Italy in general.

By the end of the Middle Ages, the prosperity of Italian city-states led to the employment of large numbers of mercenaries, as these towns constantly fought against each other. Pike-armed mercenaries from Switzerland became especially valued in these conflicts, and the Swiss Way of War was born.

Louis II de la Trémoille carefully set up his troop dispositions and then decided to sit back and rest ahead of a battle that he was confident would be on his terms. The Swiss, never conventional fighters, caught him off guard, however.

LOCATION

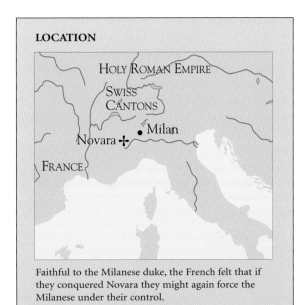

Faithful to the Milanese duke, the French felt that if they conquered Novara they might again force the Milanese under their control.

The French involvement in Italian affairs stretched back into the previous century when Charles VIII (1483–1498) had been invited by the Milanese to lay claim to the kingdom of Naples. Charles quickly lost whatever Italian prizes he had won, but his successor Louis XII (1498–1515) soon returned to the campaign trail south of the Alps, and enjoyed considerable success. However, despite victory at Ravenna in 1512, the French were chased out of Milan the following month, and in 1513 the French general Louis II de la Trémoille settled for the more modest goal of laying siege to the smaller town of Novara.

At this time Novara was held by mercenaries of the Swiss Confederation, and La Trémoille, keen to engineer battle conditions most favorable to his own army, marched out to a field about a couple of miles away from his siege lines, where he encamped for the night, expecting the Swiss to do battle with him the following morning. The Swiss, however, were unconventional fighters, who prided themselves on not doing the "expected" thing and decided to surprise the French with a night attack, hoping

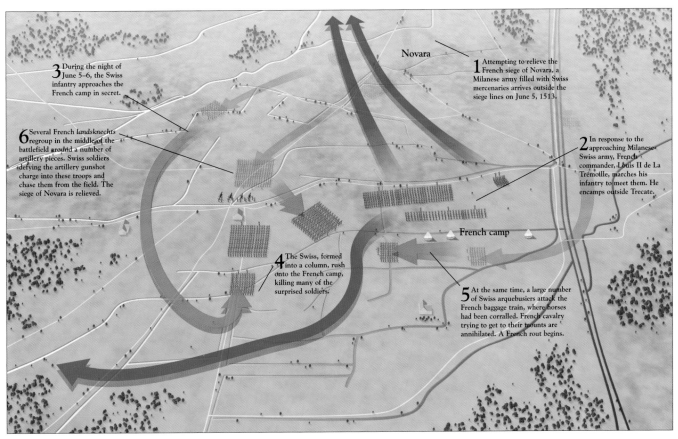

The French Valois kings dreamt of taking control of large areas of Italy. Milan was one of its richest cities, but gaining control of Novara was crucial before their plans to take it could be further implemented.

to catch many of the French asleep or at least unprepared to fight a battle.

The Swiss Army was almost entirely made up of infantry soldiers, pikemen, polearmers and arquebusiers. Of the 8,000–9,000 troops, only about 200 were Milanese cavalry. These units marched quietly to the battlefield, trying not to arouse any French scouts or pickets. Arriving outside the camp undetected, the infantry rushed onto the sleeping Frenchmen. La Trémoille's army was entirely surprised. On the left, the Swiss were able to sweep around the camp and the town of Trecate, to fall onto the virtually unprotected French baggage train. The right column came out of the woods and set upon the French cavalry, who were confused and unable to mount any resistance. The arquebusiers in this contingent simply fired round after round of gunshot into the cavalry until they were killed or had fled. The remaining soldiers in this column performed their own flanking attack, joining their middle column in an assault on the French camp.

However, it was the large center column of the Swiss that did the most damage to the French, whose tents were quickly overrun. Many French soldiers immediately fled in rout. But a large number of *landsknechts* (German mercenaries) regrouped in a defensive line near Trecate, positioning their artillery – which seems largely to have survived the initial attacks – in front of them. The Swiss, too, had regrouped into their columns and, defying the artillery barrage, charged. Contemporary reports, including one written by Florange de la Marck, the commander of the French *landsknechts,* claim that a volley of cannonballs mowed through the Swiss. It did not stop them and, before a second volley could be fired, they were upon the *landsknechts,* killing and wounding with a ruthlessness fitting their reputation. It was over quickly.

As for La Trémoille, it seems he had fled at the initial Swiss attack. Most historians have thus branded him a coward, although some have claimed that he was merely trying to set up a cavalry counter-attack. If so, it never materialized. In fact, most of his cavalry fled with him. Almost all of the French cavalry got away, with only about 40 losing their lives, while more than 5,000 infantry lay dead or dying on the battlefield.

TIMELINE

1500–1000BC	1000–500BC	500BC–0AD	0–500AD	500–1000AD	1000–1500AD	1500–2000AD

Pavia 1525

KEY FACTS

WHO The French army led by King Francis I (1515–1547) against the Spanish imperial army under the command of Charles de Lannoy.

WHAT The Imperialist forces caught those of the French in the huge hunting park of Mirabello just outside the city walls, and effectively crushed them.

WHERE Pavia, Lombardy, northern Italy.

WHEN February 24, 1525

WHY The French had lost their territories in Lombardy, and Francis I was determined to regain them, bringing him into conflict with the ascendant power of the Spanish Hapsburg ruler Charles V.

OUTCOME The French king was taken prisoner and forced to sign the Treaty of Madrid, surrendering his claims to Italian territories to Spain.

Francis I was one of the more successful French monarchs on the battlefield and something of a chivalric throwback to previous centuries. But he met his match at Pavia in 1525, when a heavy defeat by the Imperial army of Spain led to his own capture and the near-wipeout of his army.

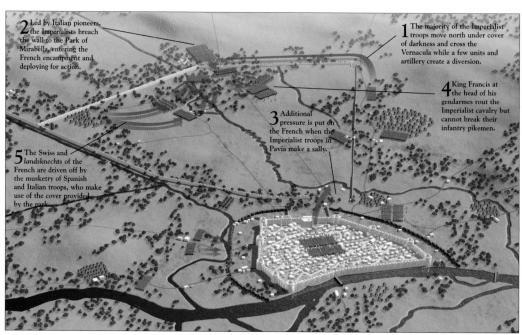

2 Led by Italian pioneers, the Imperialists breach the wall to the Park of Mirabella, entering the French encampment and deploying for action.

1 The majority of the Imperialist troops move north under cover of darkness and cross the Vernacula while a few units and artillery create a diversion.

4 King Francis at the head of his gendarmes rout the Imperialist cavalry but cannot break their infantry pikemen.

3 Additional pressure is put on the French when the Imperialist troops in Pavia make a sally.

5 The Swiss and landsknechts of the French are driven off by the musketry of Spanish and Italian troops, who make use of the cover provided by the park.

A ducal hunting park sounds like an unusually idyllic setting for a battle but, surrounded by woods ideal for concealing advancing artillery, it proved to be a trap for Francis I's army.

LOCATION

AUSTRIA

FRANCE

Milan • ✚ Pavia • Venice

PAPAL STATES

Naples •

King Francis I of France laid siege to Pavia in 1524. The purpose was to secure his lines of communication before proceeding to attack Naples.

Francis I had crossed the Alps at the head of a huge army in the autumn of 1524, determined to revive his predecessors' dreams of conquering Milan and the kingdom of Naples. But when he laid siege to the Lombard city of Pavia, a Spanish Imperial army under the command of Charles de Lannoy launched an attack after breaching the wall of the ducal hunting park used by the French as their camp. As the Imperial forces entered the park and deployed into battle order, the garrison within the city also sallied forwards. Caught by surprise, Francis was forced to commit his forces in uncoordinated attacks on several fronts.

Using the concealment provided by nearby woods, the Imperialist forces were able to hide the location of much of their infantry, both pikemen and arquebusiers, which enabled them to be used to maximum effect while securing minimal casualties themselves. Francis I himself fought valiantly on until his horse was killed under him. Surrounded by arquebusiers, he was eventually taken prisoner. The captured king's letter home to his mother – "All is lost save honour" – summed up the extent of the French debacle.

TIMELINE

1500–1000BC	1000–500BC	500BC–0AD	0–500AD	500–1000AD	1000–1500AD	1500–2000AD

Mohács 1526

King Louis II of Hungary and Bohemia was only 20 at the Battle of Mohács—the same age, in fact, as Alexander the Great when he won his first great battle. Unfortunately, Louis was no Alexander, and his army was blown away by the Turks in a chilling demonstration of the use of artillery.

KEY FACTS

WHO Ottoman army led by Suleiman the Magnificent, against Hungarian army under King Louis II.

WHAT Rather foolishly, the feeble army of the Hungarians attempted to confront the might of the Ottoman Turks and their formidable artillery, and were predictably blown away in the space of a couple of hours.

WHERE Mohács, near Budapest, Hungary.

WHEN August 29, 1526

WHY Suleiman the Magnificent saw Hungary as a stepping stone for a deeper Turkish advance into Europe.

OUTCOME After their defeat at Mohács, the days of an independent Hungary were at an end as it was contested and carved up between the Ottomans and Austrians.

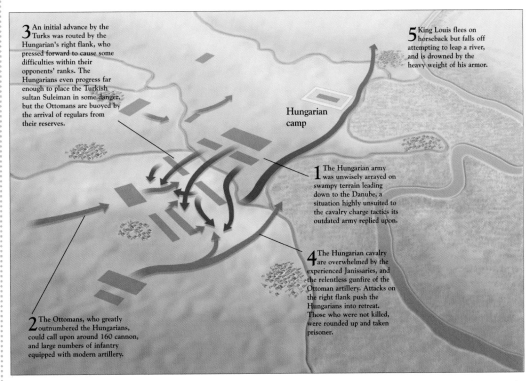

3 An initial advance by the Turks was routed by the Hungarian's right flank, who pressed forward to cause some difficulties within their opponents' ranks. The Hungarians even progress far enough to place the Turkish sultan Suleiman in some danger, but the Ottomans are buoyed by the arrival of regulars from their reserves.

5 King Louis flees on horseback but falls off attempting to leap a river, and is drowned by the heavy weight of his armor.

Hungarian camp

1 The Hungarian army was unwisely arrayed on swampy terrain leading down to the Danube, a situation highly unsuited to the cavalry charge tactics its outdated army replied upon.

4 The Hungarian cavalry are overwhelmed by the experienced Janissaries, and the relentless gunfire of the Ottoman artillery. Attacks on the right flank push the Hungarians into retreat. Those who were not killed, were rounded up and taken prisoner.

2 The Ottomans, who greatly outnumbered the Hungarians, could call upon around 160 cannon, and large numbers of infantry equipped with modern artillery.

The Turkish advance through the battered borders of Eastern Europe was a cause for real concern in the early sixteenth century. The defeat of the Hungarian army at Mohács, predictable as it seems, was a catastrophe.

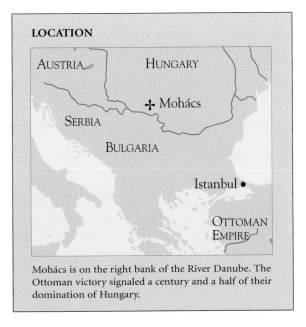

LOCATION

AUSTRIA

HUNGARY

✝ Mohács

SERBIA

BULGARIA

Istanbul •

OTTOMAN EMPIRE

Mohács is on the right bank of the River Danube. The Ottoman victory signaled a century and a half of their domination of Hungary.

By the 1520s, the Ottoman advance seemed unstoppable. Only Hungary seemed to stand in its way of moving into Europe. Louis II, king of Hungary and Bohemia, was married to a Hapsburg princess. This was a potentially dangerous alliance, so the sultan Suleiman the Magnificent decided on an invasion. Louis was determined to put up a fight, despite his army being ill-trained and out-dated, and reliant on heavily armored cavalry, in contrast to the professional Turks, fully equipped with the latest artillery.

CRUSHING LOSS

Louis chose the terrain on which to fight. While an initial attack by his right flank went well, the Ottoman guns soon begun to roll out their fire. Under such a withering onslaught, the Hungarians were shot to pieces in little more than an hour. Louis himself escaped, but his own end was near. When he was thrown from his horse as it tried to leap a river, the weight of his out-moded armor dragged him down and he drowned.

TIMELINE

1500–1000BC	1000–500BC	500BC–0AD	0–500AD	500–1000AD	1000–1500AD	1500–2000AD

Pavia

PAVIA

Francis I of France and Henry VIII of England, in youth at least, had much in common. They were a kind of throwback to the medieval age of chivalry, symbolized by their alliance at the Field of the Cloth of Gold in 1520. Francis I had ambitions to build an empire, but he was old-fashioned in another sense, in that he relied upon cavalry and footsoldiers. At Pavia he was confronted by the future—an imperial army deploying arquebusiers to maximum effect. Francis fought valiantly, but defeat was certain, and his remorseful letter home to his mother—"All is lost save honour"—has a poetic quality. But poets don't win wars, and Francis would gain more garlands as a patron of the arts.

Kawanakajima 1561

KEY FACTS

WHO	The *daimyo* army of Takada Shingen of the Kai province, against that of Uesugi Kenshin of the Echigo province.
WHAT	A battle in which the Uesugi had seemed to grab the initiative became a test of stamina—including a remarkable scuffle between the two commanders – in which the protagonists fought each other to a standstill.
WHERE	Kawanakajima, in modern-day Nagano, Japan.
WHEN	September 10, 1561
WHY	Uesugi Kenshin believed the Kai were planning an attack on his Echigo territories, and amassed a large army to forestall it.
OUTCOME	Although there was no clear winner, with both sides suffering heavy casualties, the Uesugi force withdrew from the region.

This battle was one of five clashes on the plain of Kawanakajima between 1553 and 1564. The participants in these battles remained constant – the armies of Takeda Shingen and Uesugi Kenshin, rivals for power in the Age of the Warring States.

This battle dissolved into a series of stand-offs between cavalry, bowmen, arquebusiers and footsoldiers, with the two sides fighting each other to a standstill.

LOCATION

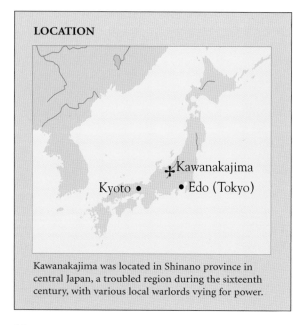

Kawanakajima was located in Shinano province in central Japan, a troubled region during the sixteenth century, with various local warlords vying for power.

The battleground sits in northern Shinano province, near the city of Nagano. Shinano separated the provinces of the warring parties—Uesugi's Echigo province in the north and Takeda's Kai province in the southeast. In September 1561, Uesugi began a large deployment of forces towards the plain of Kawanakajima, based on the expectation that Takeda was building up to a major invasion of Echigo itself. Takeda had marched out from Kai with an army of around 16,000 warriors on September 27, reaching Kawanakajima in about six days. At first, he deployed the bulk of his army on the Chausuyama heights to the west of the plain, and effectively blocked the return path for the Uesugi army.

Then, on October 8, Takeda took his force down from the Chausuyama, crossed the Chikumagawa River that ran along the western portion of the plain, and occupied the fortress in the south-eastern corner, known as Kaizu. This movement was conducted under the noses of the Uesugi, who had their forces deployed on the wooded Saijosan high ground.

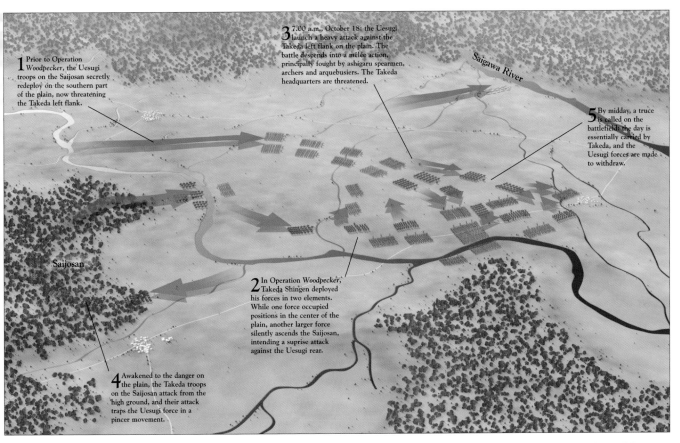

1 Prior to Operation *Woodpecker*, the Uesugi troops on the Saijosan secretly redeploy on the southern part of the plain, now threatening the Takeda left flank.

3 7.00 a.m., October 18: the Uesugi launch a heavy attack against the Takeda left flank on the plain. The battle descends into a mêlée action, principally fought by ashigaru spearmen, archers and arquebusiers. The Takeda headquarters are threatened.

Saigawa River

5 By midday, a truce is called on the battlefield: the day is essentially carried by Takeda, and the Uesugi forces are made to withdraw.

Saijosan

2 In Operation *Woodpecker*, Takeda Shingen deployed his forces in two elements. While one force occupied positions in the center of the plain, another larger force silently ascends the Saijosan, intending a suprise attack against the Uesugi rear.

4 Awakened to the danger on the plain, the Takeda troops on the Saijosan attack from the high ground, and their attack traps the Uesugi force in a pincer movement.

The Uesugi attempted to take the initiative by moving down onto the plain at night, smothering the noise of their horses' hooves with cloth. It deceived their opponents, but achieved no battle-swinging advantage.

It would surely only be a matter of time before the Uesugi began their assault. In a pre-emptive move, Takeda launched Operation *Woodpecker*. The plan ran as follows. Takeda would take out 8,000 men from Kaizu during the night, moving them silently across the Chikumagawa to the center of the plain. At the same time, a force of 12,000 soldiers was to climb the Saijosan and, when the time was right, attack the Uesugi troops there from the rear. Theoretically, the Saijosan assault would force the Uesugi men down from the mountain on to the plain, where they would be driven onto a crushing flank attack.

Operation *Woodpecker* was launched at midnight on October 18, although by this time there had already been significant movement in the Uesugi camp. At 10:00 p.m. on October 17, Uesugi had actually taken his troops down from the Saijosan in secret (even the horses' hooves were wrapped in cloth to dampen the noise), having been alerted by his scouts to the intended movements out from Kaizu. When Takeda rose the following morning, he found the Uesugi forces deployed and waiting for him, ready to do battle.

Takeda's right flank was subjected to a fast and violent assault from the Uesugi mounted samurai at around 7:00 a.m., while arquebusiers blasted out their volleys of gunshot. The Uesugi operated a winding wheel attack system, in which fresh troops were rotated into the attack as battle-tired troops moved out, so maintaining the momentum of the assault. The attack was bearing fruit, and at around 9:00 a.m. the Uesugi vanguard even closed on Takeda's headquarters, resulting in an individual combat between the two principal commanders. Uesugi received two injuries in the battle, but his bodyguard force managed to drive away Takeda and his retainers. Yet despite fearful losses, the Takeda defense held out. Furthermore, by this point the Operation *Woodpecker* detachment on the Saijosan had raced down from the mountainside and clashed with the Uesugi rearguard.

Now the Takeda plan to trap the Uesugi in a pincer movement was bearing fruit. Yet such were the level of casualties that at midday a truce was called. The Uesugi force subsequently withdrew from the battlefield, with both sides having suffered 60–70 percent casualties.

TIMELINE

1500–1000BC	1000–500BC	500BC–0AD	0–500AD	500–1000AD	1000–1500AD	1500–2000AD

Siege of Malta 1565

KEY FACTS

WHO Knights Hospitallers led by Chevalier Jean la de Vallette against a siege army of the Ottoman Empire, led by Mustafa Pasha.

WHAT The Ottomans launched a concerted effort to take the harbor fort of St Elmo, but met with spirited resistance. By the time they had stormed the fortifications, their supplies were running low, and they had lost many soldiers.

WHERE Malta.

WHEN May 18–September 11, 1565

WHY The Ottomans regarded Christian-held Malta as an obstacle to their shipping and lines of communication in the Mediterranean.

OUTCOME The Ottomans remained major players in the Mediterranean, but the failure to take Malta halted efforts to make further inroads into Europe.

How could a little island hope to hold out against the rampant Ottoman Empire? In 1565, the doughty Knights Hospitallers gave an object lesson in resistance that heartened military underdogs for centuries afterwards.

OTTOMAN–HABSBURG WARS

KNIGHTS HOSPITALLERS VICTORY

The Ottomans appeared to hold all the aces at Malta, but Mustafa Pasha was an arrogant commander, not much liked by his generals. His impatience would weaken his army's resolve and the siege would end in failure.

LOCATION

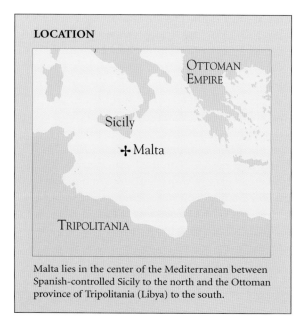

OTTOMAN EMPIRE

Sicily

✛ Malta

TRIPOLITANIA

Malta lies in the center of the Mediterranean between Spanish-controlled Sicily to the north and the Ottoman province of Tripolitania (Libya) to the south.

As the Ottoman Empire swept through the Balkans and Hungary and menaced the Mediterranean, the Order of the Hospitaller Knights of St. John held out on the rocky island of Malta, where they had been based since the fall of Rhodes in 1522 to the Turks. The order had proved a persistent and serious threat to Muslim shipping and lines of communication in the Mediterranean, and Sultan Suleiman the Magnificent was determined to crush it by invading and conquering Malta. As a strategic base in Turkish hands, the island, located south of Sicily and Naples, would be ideally suited for invading Italy and creating trouble for the infidels in the Sultan's Holy War against Christian Europe.

GRAND MASTER

But the Knights and the people of Malta had an indefatigable leader in the Grand Master of the Order, Chevalier Jean Parisot de la Vallette. As a young man, La Vallette had taken part in the siege of Rhodes and was determined to die rather than surrender Malta to an enemy he feared and loathed in equal measure.

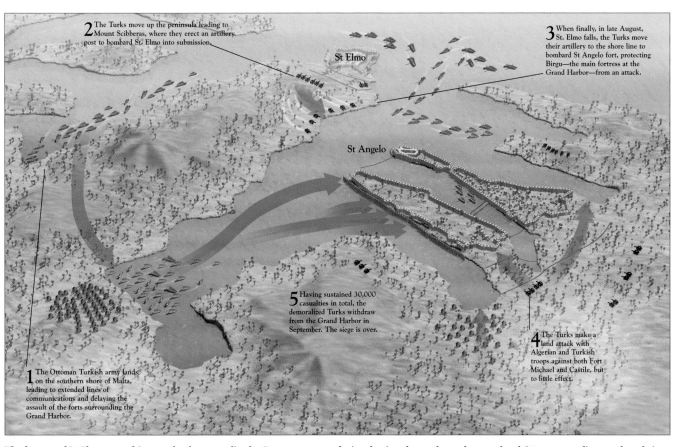

2 The Turks move up the peninsula leading to Mount Scibberas, where they erect an artillery post to bombard St. Elmo into submission.

St Elmo

3 When finally, in late August, St. Elmo falls, the Turks move their artillery to the shore line to bombard St Angelo fort, protecting Birgu—the main fortress at the Grand Harbor—from an attack.

St Angelo

5 Having sustained 30,000 casualties in total, the demoralized Turks withdraw from the Grand Harbor in September. The siege is over.

4 The Turks make a land attack with Algerian and Turkish troops against both Fort Michael and Castile, but to little effect.

1 The Ottoman Turkish army lands on the southern shore of Malta, leading to extended lines of communications and delaying the assault of the forts surrounding the Grand Harbor.

The fortress of St. Elmo was subject to relentless pounding by Ottoman cannon during the siege, but as the weeks passed and Ottoman supplies grew low, their efforts to break in became more frantic.

When the Ottomans, under the leadership of Mustafa Pasha, landed on the island, they began by attacking the fortress of St. Elmo, which protected the harbor, expecting to take it in a matter of days. The fortress's perceived weakness was its low position, making it vulnerable to artillery fire. The Turks constructed a parapet on the heights above St. Elmo and placed two 60-pounders, ten 80-pounders, and a single massive mortar that fired 160 pounds (73kg) of solid shot inside this battery. They used marble, iron and stone cannon balls to bombard the fort, but their fire made little impression.

Under relentless fire, senior officers urged the Grand Master to evacuate St. Elmo, but this only made La Vallette more determined to hold the fortress at all costs. He sacked fainthearted Knights, sent reinforcements and admonished the fort's commandant Luigi Broglia to fight to the death. La Vallette knew that every day that St. Elmo held out meant more time for the main forts—and more time for relief to arrive.

Mustafa Pasha, increasingly frantic as the weeks passed, decided to send in waves of *Iayalars,* or volunteers, armed with scimitars. Encouraged by Mullahs shouting verses out of the Koran, and supported by the fire of 4,000 musketeers, the *Iayalars* threw themselves at the walls only to be thrown back by the defenders' fire and weapons. The attack left 150 defenders dead, but also more than a thousand *Iayalars.*

By the time the Turks finally broke through a few days later, it had taken nearly one-quarter of their number – 8,000 men—to take this, the smallest and weakest of the Maltese forts. When they moved to take the larger fortresses of Birgu and Senglea, they faced similar resistance. A Turkish mine breached the walls of Birgu, and the Turks rushed through, only to face Knights and Maltese defenders led by La Vallette in person. La Vallette was wounded in the leg, but had it dressed only when the city wall was safely back in Christian hands.

Next, a massive wooden siege tower was set on fire by the Knights using their arsenal of inflammables, and after almost three months, the Turks were increasingly demoralized. By the time a small Spanish relief force had arrived, the last Turks had departed, never to return.

TIMELINE

1500–1000BC	1000–500BC	500BC–0AD	0–500AD	500–1000AD	1000–1500AD	1500–2000AD

Lepanto 1571

KEY FACTS

WHO Don Juan (John) of Austria, at the command of the Holy League fleet, against the Turkish grand admiral Ali Pasha, leading the main Ottoman fleet.

WHAT Against a Turkish fleet still largely committed to fighting sea battles by the old tactic of ramming and boarding, the greater cannon fire that the Christians brought to the fray was decisive.

WHERE Lepanto, Gulf of Patras, off western Greece coast.

WHEN October 7, 1571

WHY The pope had urged a crusade to drive off the advancing Ottoman Turks, who had conquered Cyprus and threatened to take control of the Mediterranean.

OUTCOME Despite their fleet being pounded to destruction, the Ottomans rebuilt fast and remained a major Mediterranean power.

The five-hour battle at Lepanto was the largest sea battle ever fought in the Mediterranean. And in the deployment by the Venetians of the massive galleas, a hybrid ship somewhere between a galley and a galleon, the age of the cannon broadside was born.

By the time of Lepanto, the Turks were still deploying old-style ramming and boarding tactics, and their vessels proved vulnerable against the guns of the Christian allies.

LOCATION

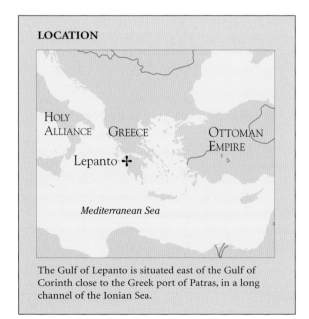

HOLY ALLIANCE GREECE OTTOMAN EMPIRE

Lepanto ✛

Mediterranean Sea

The Gulf of Lepanto is situated east of the Gulf of Corinth close to the Greek port of Patras, in a long channel of the Ionian Sea.

By the middle of the sixteenth century, the Ottomans were threatening to take control in the waters of the western Mediterranean. In 1571, the Venetians were in danger of losing the vital port and outpost of Cyprus when Pope Pius V proclaimed a crusade against the Turks. There was not much time to be lost in mobilizing the Christian response—a powerful Turkish fleet was poised to enter the Adriatic Sea.

The fleet the Venetians dispatched to Lepanto would be the largest in the Republic's history, and the best equipped, able to call upon big new ships known as galleasses, specially built to hold the largest cannon available from the Republic's stockpiles. These ships could fire some 325 lb (147kg) of shot in every salvo – equivalent to the cannon firepower of five standard galleys of the time. The galleass was, quite literally, a castle on the sea, and it required four smaller vessels to tow them forward. Alongside them was a new and formidable Spanish fleet, under the command of Emperor Philip of Spain's bastard brother, Don Juan of Austria.

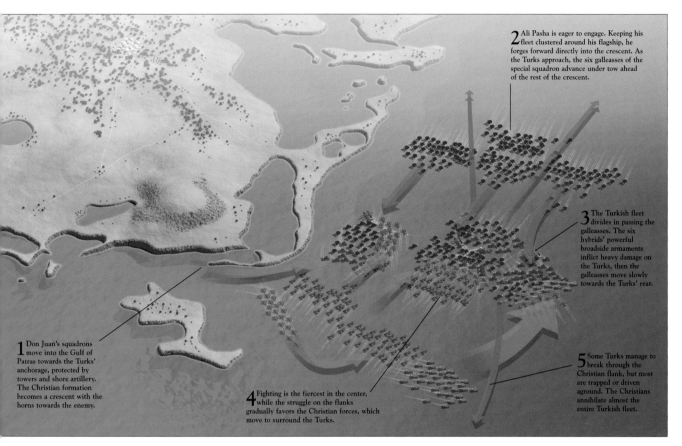

2 Ali Pasha is eager to engage. Keeping his fleet clustered around his flagship, he forges forward directly into the crescent. As the Turks approach, the six galleasses of the special squadron advance under tow ahead of the rest of the crescent.

3 The Turkish fleet divides in passing the galleasses. The six hybrids' powerful broadside armaments inflict heavy damage on the Turks, then the galleasses move slowly towards the Turks' rear.

1 Don Juan's squadrons move into the Gulf of Patras towards the Turks' anchorage, protected by towers and shore artillery. The Christian formation becomes a crescent with the horns towards the enemy.

4 Fighting is the fiercest in the center, while the struggle on the flanks gradually favors the Christian forces, which move to surround the Turks.

5 Some Turks manage to break through the Christian flank, but most are trapped or driven aground. The Christians annihilate almost the entire Turkish fleet.

Not only did the Christian allies have greater artillery power on their ships, but they were also able to deploy guns on the shores. The Turkish fleet was effectively annihilated by the combined firepower.

As Ali Pasha, the Turkish grand admiral, methodically collected his forces in the Gulf of Patras on the western coast of Greece, the Christian fleet moved slowly eastwards and the two adversaries met off the Greek coast around Lepanto.

Ali Pasha noted the six large vessels – the galleasses – set out as the vanguard of the Christian line and chose to bypass them by ordering his three squadrons to divide and sail around them without engaging. But long-range fire from the broadsides of the galleasses added to the disorder of the Turkish squadrons as they passed. The situation became worse as the Christians moved to engage before the Turkish fleet could reform, and any hope of avoiding the terrible firepower of the galleasses proved vain as the lumbering monsters reversed direction and fell upon the Turkish rear.

The Turkish efforts to reform were not assisted by the clouds of smoke resulting from the cannon of both sides and from the arquebuses with which the crewmen on the Spanish fleet were armed. The Turks were accurate and proficient archers, but matchlocks provided a counter to their arrows. Light artillery pieces on swivels—called versos, or murderers—poured fire onto the Turkish decks.

The galleasses' great height of their wooden sides rendered them practically immune to Turkish efforts to board them. The goal of both fleets was to envelop the other, and fierce fighting raged on the flanks of each line. Gunpowder and thick armor began to make a difference in the Christians' favor. As the Turkish marines perished, another calamity befell their ships. The Christian slaves on the benches of the Turkish fleet began availing themselves of weapons dropped in the carnage and attacked their former masters. While the ships were so embroiled, they lost all propulsion and hope of maneuver or escape.

When the day ended, 7,700 Christians and 12 ships had sunk beneath the reddened waters of the gulf. By contrast, some 30,000 Turks had perished in the carnage and 170 galleys and lighter vessels of the Turkish fleet had been captured. That the galleasses had played a huge part, no one doubted. The West's faith in technology had been amply vindicated at Lepanto.

TIMELINE

1500–1000BC	1000–500BC	500BC–0AD	0–500AD	500–1000AD	1000–1500AD	1500–2000AD

Nagashino 1575

KEY FACTS

WHO The daimyo (feudal lord) Takeda Katsuyori (1546–82) fought the combined forces of Oda Nobunaga (1534–82) and Tokugawa Ieyasu (1543–1616).

WHAT Takeda besieged Nagashino Castle, to which Oda and Tokugawa sent a massive relief army that was heavily armed with arquebus gunners.

WHERE The area around Nagashino Castle, in Totomi Province, central Japan.

WHEN June 28, 1575

WHY Takeda had wider territorial ambitions for central Japan and was aiming to defeat the Tokugawa armies and advance against Kyoto.

OUTCOME An eight-hour battle saw the almost complete destruction of Takeda's army, with devastating casualties caused by volley fire from enemy arquebusiers.

The Battle of Nagashino was a clash of old and new technologies. The traditional Japanese "way of the sword" confronted the reality of early firearms, with decisive results that were to change the way battles were fought in Japan.

Traditional samurai fighting tactics still had a part to play at Nagashino, but by this era artillery and musketry were becoming the decisive factors in warfare.

LOCATION

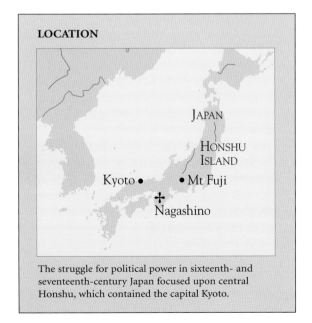

JAPAN

HONSHU ISLAND

Kyoto • • Mt Fuji

✚
Nagashino

The struggle for political power in sixteenth- and seventeenth-century Japan focused upon central Honshu, which contained the capital Kyoto.

The Battle of Nagashino took place on a soggy plain some 3.1 miles (5km) from the castle, behind the banks of the Rengogawa River. A three-tiered palisade of wooden stakes just high enough to prevent a horse jumping over was also built a short distance behind the river. Along with the wet ground, this would hamper a cavalry charge, and it also provided cover for Oda Nobunaga's arquebusiers.

Both sides at the Battle of Nagashino used firearms, but it was Oda, drawing on his brutal past experience, who best understood the tactical applications of such weapons. The arquebus, a simple muzzle-lock loaded firearm, had been introduced into Japan from Portugal in 1543. However, while it was light enough to fire from the shoulder, it had nothing in the way of sights, and accuracy was poor: its range was limited to a few hundred metres, misfires were frequent and reloading was laborious. What Oda understood, however, was its great value as a weapon when used in volley. Furthermore, handling an arquebus required a fraction

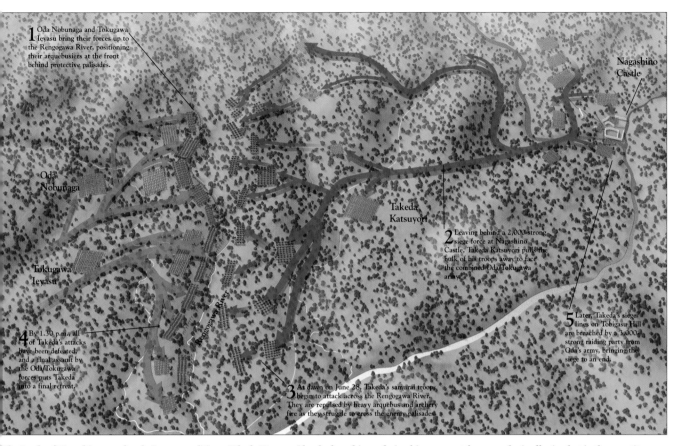

1 Oda Nobunaga and Tokugawa Ieyasu bring their forces up to the Rengogawa River, positioning their arquebusiers at the front behind protective palisades.

Oda Nobunaga

Tokugawa Ieyasu

Rengogawa River

4 By 1.30 p.m., all of Takeda's attacks have been defeated, and a final assault by the Oda/Tokugawa forces puts Takeda into a final retreat.

Takeda Katsuyori

2 Leaving behind a 2,000-strong siege force at Nagashino Castle, Takeda Katsuyori pulls the bulk of his troops away to face the combined Oda/Tokugawa army.

Nagashino Castle

5 Later, Takeda's siege lines on Tobigasu Hill are breached by a 3,000-strong raiding party from Oda's army, bringing the siege to an end.

3 At dawn on June 28, Takeda's samurai troops begin to attack across the Rengogawa River. They are repulsed by heavy arquebus and archery fire as they struggle to cross the enemy palisades.

The Battle of Nagashino was fought in wet conditions. Takeda Katsuyori banked on this rendering his opponents' gunpowder ineffective, but in the event it was his old-fashioned cavalry who were disadvantaged by having to charge through mud.

of the skill demanded of a bowman, enabling an army to rapidly increase its firepower.

VOLLEY TACTICS

Oda took 3,000 arquebusiers with him to the Nagashino battlefield, and trained them in the application of disciplined volley tactics. During the lulls in reloading, archers would take over to maintain a constant rain of direct fire on the enemy. Takeda also had arquebus-armed troops, but at the time of Nagashino he still relied on cavalry dash. This tactical decision proved to be his ondoing.

When Oda's army arrived on the plain, Takeda, instead of maintaining a defensive position by the castle, opted for military glory by charging across open ground to meet him. Wiser commanders had counseled against this, fearing it would leave them vulnerable to sustaining heavy casualties from ball and arrow. But Takeda opted for a full-frontal attack on Oda's dispositions because he'd surmised that the enemy arquebuses would prove useless because of wet weather. In fact, the arquebusiers'

powder had been kept dry, and the principal effect of the rain was to make the terrain even more ill-suited to a fast cavalry charge.

As the horsemen emerged up the far bank, a withering fusillade of fire rippled out from Oda's matchlockmen, arranged behind the palisade in three ranks, each rank, firing in turn. Some 9,000 rounds were fired in the first three rapid volleys alone, and cavalrymen and horses dropped in horrifying numbers as shot hit their targets from around 55 yards (50m).

CHANGING FACE OF BATTLE

Much bloody hand-to-hand combat, using the traditional samurai sword and spear, did take place, and the fact that the battle raged for eight hours before Takeda finally withdrew his men from the fray suggests that the weaponry of bow, sword and spear still played a major part. Nevertheless, the arquebus had been central to Oda's conclusive victory, causing a high level of casualties and dealing a crushing blow to a force relying on traditional methods of warfare.

TIMELINE

1500–1000BC	1000–500BC	500BC–0AD	0–500AD	500–1000AD	1000–1500AD	1500–2000AD

Gravelines 1588

Long-standing tension between Protestant England and Catholic Spain turned into open war in 1585. In July 1588, the Spanish fleet entered the English Channel, intending to invade the British Isles.

KEY FACTS

WHO A Spanish fleet of 22 galleons and 108 armed merchant vessels under the Duke of Medina Sidonia, opposed by an English fleet comprised of 35 galleons and 163 other vessels and commanded by the Lord High Admiral, Charles Howard.

WHAT The Spanish intended to invade England in conjunction with a Dutch-based army, who were to be transported by the Armada from the Spanish Netherlands.

WHERE A series of running engagements in the English Channel, with a decisive battle off Gravelines near the Belgian coast.

WHEN July and August 1588

WHY Ongoing conflict between Protestant England and Catholic Spain, largely due to religious differences.

OUTCOME The Spanish fleet was defeated off Gravelines and was forced to sail north around Britain to return home.

The Spanish galleons looked magnificent – with high "castles" like siege towers at the stern and the grandeur of floating fortresses. But the sleeker English ships were built for carrying cannon and were more suited to battle on the open sea.

LOCATION

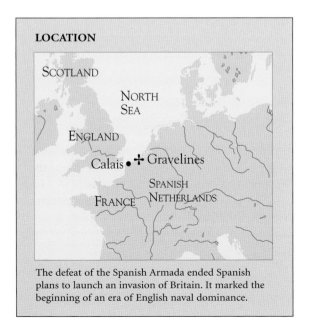

The defeat of the Spanish Armada ended Spanish plans to launch an invasion of Britain. It marked the beginning of an era of English naval dominance.

The Spanish Armada sailed on England in May 1588. By July, it was sailing off the Cornish coast, but for some time afterwards nothing more than a series of indecisive engagements occurred. However, when the Duke of Medina Sidonia was unable to anchor the fleet in the sheltered waters of the Isle of Wight due to harrying by several English ships, he sailed across the Channel to the region of northern France, anchoring off Dunkirk. This meant his ships were unprotected by a harbor, and Admiral Lord Howard, commanding the English, ordered a fireship attack – vessels carrying barrels of gunpowder and loaded with a highly combustible mix of tar and pitch were sent downwind against the Spanish force.

This threw the Spanish fleet into disarray. Although part of Spain's fleet remained in formation, large numbers of vessels were forced to cut their cables, causing great confusion. It also meant the Armada was being driven from its anchorage into open waters, where the lighter, narrower, faster English ships – designed like mobile artillery platforms, in contrast to the old-fashioned

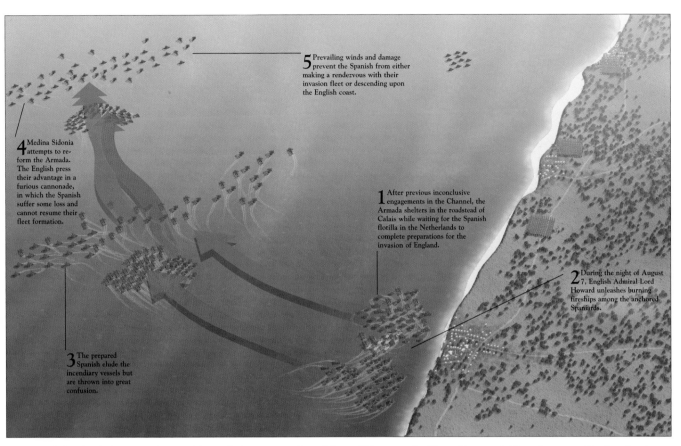

5 Prevailing winds and damage prevent the Spanish from either making a rendezvous with their invasion fleet or descending upon the English coast.

4 Medina Sidonia attempts to re-form the Armada. The English press their advantage in a furious cannonade, in which the Spanish suffer some loss and cannot resume their fleet formation.

1 After previous inconclusive engagements in the Channel, the Armada shelters in the roadstead of Calais while waiting for the Spanish flotilla in the Netherlands to complete preparations for the invasion of England.

2 During the night of August 7, English Admiral Lord Howard unleashes burning fireships among the anchored Spaniards.

3 The prepared Spanish elude the incendiary vessels but are thrown into great confusion.

The Spanish fleet faced adverse weather conditions, a furious cannonade, and the terrifying scenario of incendiary vessels. These factors combined to give victory to the English at Gravelines.

Spanish warships, with their high "castles" fore and aft like floating siege towers – would have an advantage. As the Armada struggled to regain its formation, it was blown eastwards by the winds. Off Gravelines, it was forced to halt as the Dutch coast became extremely hazardous at this point. Now the English had a chance to fight a decisive action, getting in close to fire where previous long-range bombardment had been ineffective.

To have a chance of penetrating the Spanish ships' thick hulls, the English had to fire from within a range of 100m (109yd), but this was risky since the Spanish wanted to draw their enemies in close in order to grapple and board. However, by maintaining an advantageous windward position, and by means of good seamanship, the English were able to close in, pound the Spanish and then retire to a safe distance.

Spanish gunnery was largely ineffective for several reasons. Their guns were made of bronze and fired more slowly than the English iron guns, and their crews were not well trained. The Spanish were still geared to the old idea of ships primarily being used to carry large contingents of soldiers. Cannonfire would be used sparingly, to force their opponent on the defensive, preparing the way for the anticipated grappling and boarding battle. Against some foes, this was effective, but the English ships were too manoeuvrable to be caught this way. In addition to its tactical disadvantages, the Spaniards' leeward position meant that penetrating hits often occurred below the waterline when the vessel was not heeling over towards the wind, and their guns were pointing at the sky much of the time for the same reason.

Estimates of the losses at Gravelines vary, though no more than 11 Spanish ships were lost in the battle. Many more were damaged, and the Armada was driven into the North Sea, where the English, though almost out of ammunition, pursued them as far as the Firth of Forth in Scotland. At the time, it was not clear in England that the threat had passed. An English army was mustered at Tilbury in case of an invasion up the Thames, and Queen Elizabeth I herself visited this army to deliver an inspiring speech. In the event, the encouragement was not needed. The threat of invasion had been averted.

TIMELINE

1500–1000BC	1000–500BC	500BC–0AD	0–500AD	500–1000AD	1000–1500AD	1500–2000AD

Gravelines

GRAVELINES

The sight of the Spanish Armada would have been enough to send the fleet of most nations of the sixteenth century scuttling for port. Their ships were built like floating fortresses. They put to sea with the full wind of an empire in their sails. But the English ships were sleeker affairs, gunboats of a later prototype and easier to handle. "God blew and they were scattered" read the inscriptions on commemorative medals struck to mark the way English ships had blasted their way to victory at Gravelines. The shattered remnants of the Spanish fleet were left to limp back home.

Sacheon 1592

KEY FACTS

WHO Japanese naval forces, under ultimate command of Toyotomi Hideyoshi (1536–98), were confronted by the smaller but more modern Korean fleet under Admiral Yi Sun-shin (1545–98).

WHAT Admiral Yi attacked a Japanese naval squadron anchored at Sacheon, drawing it out to sea, where he had the advantage of manoeuvrability and superior naval gunnery.

WHERE Sacheon, on the southern coast of the Korean Peninsula.

WHEN May 29, 1592

WHY With Korean land forces being routed by the Japanese, Admiral Yi chose a strategy of interdicting the Japanese maritime supply routes.

OUTCOME Up to 40 Japanese ships lost for no Korean vessels, and the beginning of Korean naval supremacy in the Imjin War (1592–98).

By neglecting the development of an effective navy, Japan was courting disaster in its invasion of Korea in 1592. At Sacheon the Korean navy, armed with groundbreaking "turtle ships," undermined the entire Japanese enterprise.

IMJIN WAR

KOREAN VICTORY

The kobukson, or "turtle" ship, was an alarming sight when unleashed on the Japanese fleet. The smoky billows from its dragon's head were scary enough, but so too was its enhanced firepower, thanks to extra gunports.

LOCATION

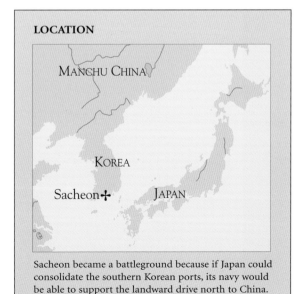

Sacheon became a battleground because if Japan could consolidate the southern Korean ports, its navy would be able to support the landward drive north to China.

Toyotomi Hideyoshi, a Japanese daimyo (feudal lord) with ambitions to conquer China, had launched an invasion of Korea when it refused a request that his army be granted free passage through the kingdom. The Japanese army had readily embraced the relatively new use of firearms by this time, and its military capabilities vastly outstripped those of Korea, who still relied on long-range composite bows as their direct-fire weapons. But as a naval power Korea was less of a pushover, thanks to the efforts of Admiral Yi Sun-shin, and had invested in new naval technology, including long range cannon, sited to give all-round (360°) fire capability.

It is true that the Japanese had more ships, but these were too lightweight for such heavy gunnery, and their crews relied on musketry, and the old marine methods of grappling, boarding and on-deck fighting, for taking control of enemy ships.

As the Japanese land forces were pushing northwards, Admiral Yi saw that they were acutely reliant upon naval logistics to fuel their advance, and began to interdict supply

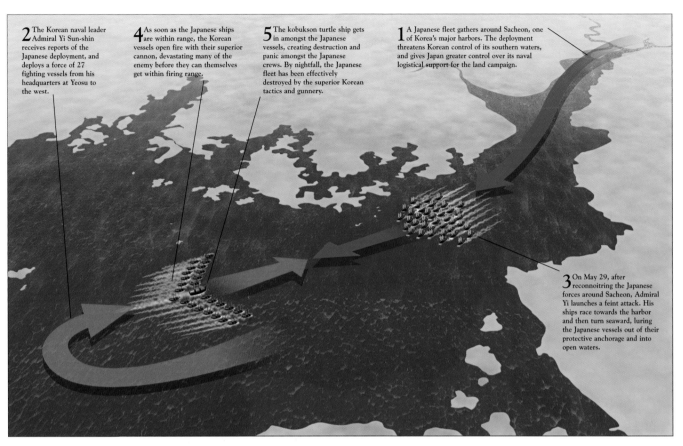

2 The Korean naval leader Admiral Yi Sun-shin receives reports of the Japanese deployment, and deploys a force of 27 fighting vessels from his headquarters at Yeosu to the west.

4 As soon as the Japanese ships are within range, the Korean vessels open fire with their superior cannon, devastating many of the enemy before they can themselves get within firing range.

5 The kobukson turtle ship gets in amongst the Japanese vessels, creating destruction and panic amongst the Japanese crews. By nightfall, the Japanese fleet has been effectively destroyed by the superior Korean tactics and gunnery.

1 A Japanese fleet gathers around Sacheon, one of Korea's major harbors. The deployment threatens Korean control of its southern waters, and gives Japan greater control over its naval logistical support for the land campaign.

3 On May 29, after reconnoitring the Japanese forces around Sacheon, Admiral Yi launches a feint attack. His ships race towards the harbor and then turn seaward, luring the Japanese vessels out of their protective anchorage and into open waters.

The "false" retreat wasn't simply deployed in land battles. It worked at sea, too. At Sacheon, the Japanese were lured to their doom by an outnumbered, but shrewdly commanded, Korean navy.

routes. Several naval engagements went as planned by Yi, and the scene was set for the Battle of Sacheon, when he led a force of 26 warships against up to 70 Japanese ships.

Yi needed to draw the Japanese out from the harbor at Sacheon to the open sea, where he would have the advantage in gunnery. To lure them, he had his force sail at speed towards the harbor, then reverse direction, as if suddenly alarmed by the sight of the Japanese warships. The Japanese fell for the ruse, and dispatched up to 40 vessels for a pursuit action. It would be a fatal mistake. The deployment took time, hence the light was fading even as the Japanese put to sea.

Once the Japanese ships were out of the harbor, the Koreans went into action, turning rapidly and using their oars to drive their ships quickly into gunnery range. Korean gunners were taught to begin engaging as soon as they entered cannon range, and soon the Japanese ships were being smashed by shot and arrows. The Japanese could respond only with peppering arquebus shots. One such shot might have changed the course of the entire war when it struck Yi, but the ball did nothing more than deliver a flesh wound to the admiral's left arm.

Now the Koreans played their ace card, launching a kobukson, or "turtle ship," a new type of warship whose firepower was delivered from around a dozen cannon ports each side of the hull, and from further ports at the stem and stern. The bow also featured a carved dragon's head, from which pumped a sulphurous smoke, serving both to lay down a screen and as a weapon of psychological warfare. The turtle ship sailed into the heart of the Japanese fleet, its cannon delivering crushing broadsides against the lightweight enemy vessels while Japanese musket balls bounced harmlessly off the upper deck and thick hull. The appearance of the kobukson caused panic. Its unusual layout and heavy firepower startled the Japanese sailors and marines, who struggled to see how the ship could be taken and were alarmed at the grinning, smoking dragon's head. By nightfall, every Japanese warship that had sailed out to engage the Koreans was sinking or critically damaged. On the Korean side, casualties amounted to just a handful of sailors injured.

TIMELINE

1500–1000BC	1000–500BC	500BC–0AD	0–500AD	500–1000AD	1000–1500AD	1500–2000AD

Hansando Island 1592

KEY FACTS

Who Korean admiral Yi Sun-shin (1545–98) faced the fleet of Toyotomi Hideyoshi (1536–98).

What Admiral Yi destroyed a large fleet of Japanese ships in open waters off the island, resulting in the death of 8,000 Japanese sailors.

Where East coast of Hansando Island, (in modern South Korea).

When August 15, 1592

Why Japanese land forces were taking control of Korea's cities, but Admiral Yi recognized they were more vulnerable at sea.

Outcome Another win despite the odds for the Korean navy against the larger forces of the Japanese, and one that ended Toyotomi Hideyoshi's over-arching dream of invading China.

At Hansando Island, the seemingly superior Japanese would once again be outwitted by the Korean Admiral Yi Sun-shin, this time in a sea battle that would end Japanese hopes of launching a full-scale invasion of China.

IMJIN WAR

KOREAN VICTORY

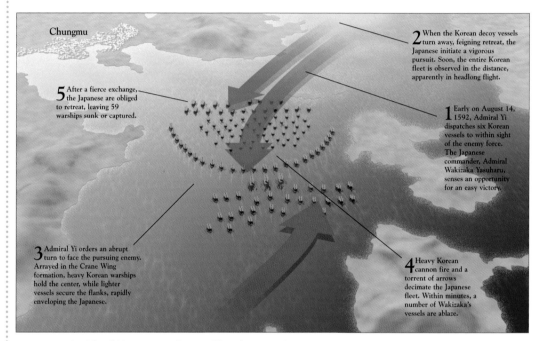

Chungmu

2 When the Korean decoy vessels turn away, feigning retreat, the Japanese initiate a vigorous pursuit. Soon, the entire Korean fleet is observed in the distance, apparently in headlong flight.

5 After a fierce exchange, the Japanese are obliged to retreat, leaving 59 warships sunk or captured.

1 Early on August 14, 1592, Admiral Yi dispatches six Korean vessels to within sight of the enemy force. The Japanese commander, Admiral Wakizaka Yasuharu, senses an opportunity for an easy victory.

3 Admiral Yi orders an abrupt turn to face the pursuing enemy. Arrayed in the Crane Wing formation, heavy Korean warships hold the center, while lighter vessels secure the flanks, rapidly enveloping the Japanese.

4 Heavy Korean cannon fire and a torrent of arrows decimate the Japanese fleet. Within minutes, a number of Wakizaka's vessels are ablaze.

Japanese territorial ambitions were undermined by inferior naval resources. Once again, at Hansando, the Koreans managed to out-maneuver them, by luring them into deep waters where more up-to-date gunships could pick them off.

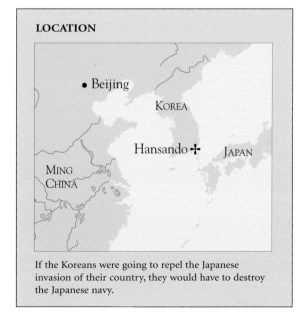

LOCATION

• Beijing

KOREA

Hansando ✛   JAPAN

MING CHINA

If the Koreans were going to repel the Japanese invasion of their country, they would have to destroy the Japanese navy.

Warned that a powerful Japanese naval force was approaching, Admiral Yi marshalled the forces of the Korean navy north of the Kyonnaeryang Strait to protect the shipping lanes in the Yellow Sea.

Admiral Yi was aware that the waters where the Japanese had paused were too shallow for his own warships. So he devised a scheme to lure the enemy away from the shoals surrounding Hansando Island and into the open sea, where his heavier panokseon ships and artillery could wreak havoc on the lighter Japanese craft. The Japanese lacked the artillery power of their enemy, whose ships were armed with cannon, and they still had to rely on old marine warfare techniques such as grappling and boarding. While some Japanese ships did get close enough to their opponents to enable this to happen, Yi was largely successful in ensuring that this happened only to Korean ships that were already crippled. Of the 73 Japanese ships deployed, 59 were damaged or sunk, while the Koreans suffered only minor damage to a number of ships. This crushing victory once again proved the superiority of Korean naval weaponry, especially the panokseon ships, as well as Korean tactics.

TIMELINE

1500–1000BC	1000–500BC	500BC–0AD	0–500AD	500–1000AD	1000–1500AD	1500–2000AD

Siege of Jinju 1593

KEY FACTS

WHO Japanese army against the Korean soldiers and civilians defending the castle of Jinju.

WHAT The Korean defenders were able to resist for 10 days against their assailants, but Japanese sappers used a camouflaged armored cart to finally make a breach in the walls.

WHERE Jinju in the Jeolla province of Korea (now South Gyeongsang province, South Korea).

WHEN July 1593

WHY Jinju was a key fortress guarding the Jeolla province of Korea.

OUTCOME Once the breach was made, the garrison commander and the entire population defending the fortress, both soldiers and civilians, were put to the sword.

The first siege of Jinju, a year before, had resulted in a Korean victory, but when the Japanese returned, their use of an unusual turtle shell armored cart helped ensure a more favorable outcome for them.

JAPANESE INVASIONS OF KOREA

JAPANESE VICTORY

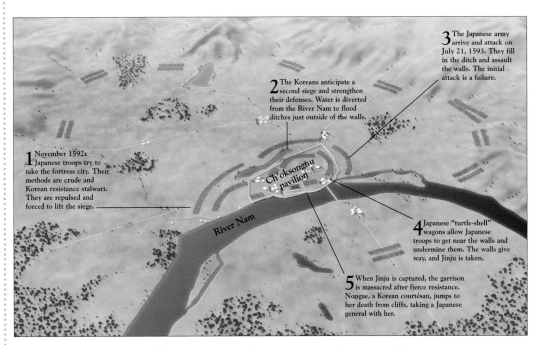

1 November 1592: Japanese troops try to take the fortress city. Their methods are crude and Korean resistance stalwart. They are repulsed and forced to lift the siege.

2 The Koreans anticipate a second siege and strengthen their defenses. Water is diverted from the River Nam to flood ditches just outside of the walls.

3 The Japanese army arrive and attack on July 21, 1593. They fill in the ditch and assault the walls. The initial attack is a failure.

4 Japanese "turtle-shell" wagons allow Japanese troops to get near the walls and undermine them. The walls give way, and Jinju is taken.

5 When Jinju is captured, the garrison is massacred after fierce resistance. Nongae, a Korean courtesan, jumps to her death from cliffs, taking a Japanese general with her.

Ch'oksonghu pavilion

River Nam

Jinju was in the heart of guerrilla fighting territory. Stealth came naturally to fighting men of the area, but the subterfuge involved in the use of a turtle shell wagon to undermine the fortress's defenses was ingenious.

LOCATION

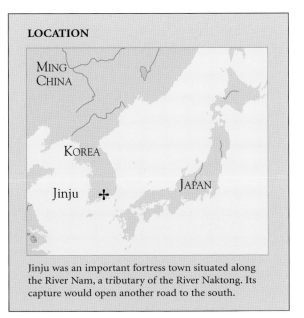

MING CHINA

KOREA

JAPAN

Jinju

Jinju was an important fortress town situated along the River Nam, a tributary of the River Naktong. Its capture would open another road to the south.

By the autumn of 1592, the Japanese invaders had achieved great success on the Korean peninsula. However, Korean partisan fighters were making life increasingly difficult for the invasion force. Jinju was a fortified city that was on the fringe of Korean guerrilla territory in Jeolla Province. By capturing the city, the Japanese would deny the guerrillas a base of support and also open a new road to Jeolla, which could then be conquered.

TURTLE SHELL WAGON

During a first siege of the castle in 1592, the Korean garrison had heroically beaten off all attacks, forcing the Japanese to withdraw. When they returned in 1593, Korean soldiers and civilians once again put up a stout defense, and succeeded in killing many Japanese soldiers. But after 10 days, Japanese sappers used camouflaged, armored "turtle shell" wagons to approach and undermine the walls. Eventually, a section of the wall collapsed, allowing the Japanese assault troops to storm in. Fighting was fierce with the Koreans battling to the last, but in the end the whole garrison, including its commander, was put to the sword.

TIMELINE

1500–1000BC	1000–500BC	500BC–0AD	0–500AD	500–1000AD	1000–1500AD	1500–2000AD

Nieuport 1600

WHO | The Dutch general Maurice of Nassau against the Spanish army led by Archduke Albrecht of Austria.

WHAT | Maurice found himself engaged, unintentionally, in a full-scale battle with the Spanish army, but was able to overcome the disorganized charges of the Spanish pikemen.

WHERE | Nieuport (in modern Belgium).

WHEN | July 2, 1600

WHY | Spanish pirates had based themselves in nearby Dunkirk, and preyed on Dutch trading vessels. Maurice of Nassau was ordered to clear them from the area.

OUTCOME | Although Maurice managed to defeat the Spanish, inflicting heavy losses upon them, privateers remained at large to prey upon Dutch commerce in the area.

When the Dutch general Maurice of Nassau set out to deal with some pirates based at Dunkirk in 1600, in Spanish-controlled territory, he did not expect to have to deal with a full-scale attack at Nieuport. His military expertise turned the situation in his favor, but was ultimately fruitless.

NETHERLANDS WAR OF INDEPENDENCE

DUTCH VICTORY

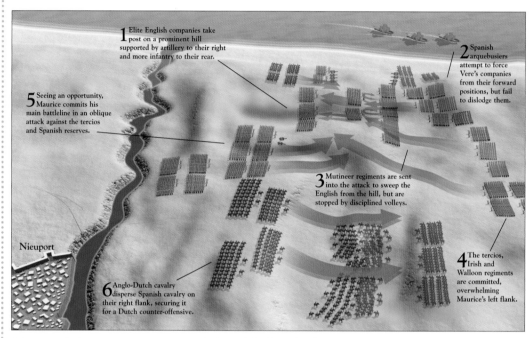

1 Elite English companies take post on a prominent hill supported by artillery to their right and more infantry to their rear.

2 Spanish arquebusiers attempt to force Vere's companies from their forward positions, but fail to dislodge them.

5 Seeing an opportunity, Maurice commits his main battleline in an oblique attack against the tercios and Spanish reserves.

3 Mutineer regiments are sent into the attack to sweep the English from the hill, but are stopped by disciplined volleys.

4 The tercios, Irish and Walloon regiments are committed, overwhelming Maurice's left flank.

6 Anglo-Dutch cavalry disperse Spanish cavalry on their right flank, securing it for a Dutch counter-offensive.

Nieuport

Privateers and pirates were a constant menace in the English Channel in this period, but a clever soldier like Maurice of Nassau would have expected to outwit them easily enough. At Nieuport, however, he had to face the Hapsburg army.

LOCATION

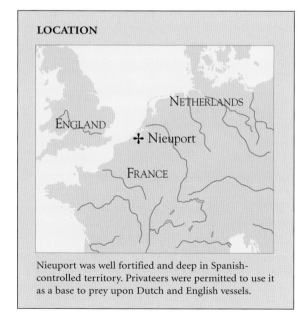

NETHERLANDS

ENGLAND

+ Nieuport

FRANCE

Nieuport was well fortified and deep in Spanish-controlled territory. Privateers were permitted to use it as a base to prey upon Dutch and English vessels.

The Dutch general Maurice of Nassau had set out to deal with Spanish privateers in Dunkirk. Mutiny was rife in the Spanish army at this period, and so he could be confident that he would reach his target without opposition. However, Albrecht of Austria moved swiftly to deploy regular Spanish troops, and Maurice soon found himself with his back to the city of Nieuport and a Spanish army across his line of supply and communications.

Archduke Albrecht began his attack with a concerted cavalry charge, soon supported by half his army, to dislodge the English companies in Maurice's employ from a forward defensive position on a hill.

Maurice responded by sending forward his main battle line. The Anglo-Dutch companies met the Spanish veterans head-on, inflicting heavy casualties. When Albrecht dispatched his reserves to the fray, it was enough to break Maurice's left but opened the Spanish oblique advance to Maurice's reserves.

Albrecht had no more troops to commit to the battle, and his cumbersome formations were assailed from both front and flank. Gradually, the Spaniards scattered in all directions, leaving their guns in the field.

TIMELINE

1500–1000BC	1000–500BC	500BC–0AD	0–500AD	500–1000AD	1000–1500AD	1500–2000AD

Sekigahara 1600

KEY FACTS

WHO The clans of Tokugawa Ieyasu's Eastern Army against those of the Western Army of Ishida Mitsunari.

WHAT The Western Army entered the battle with a well thought-out tactical plan. Secret negotiations between Tokugawa and several of Ishida's allies meant their defection at key moments in the battle contributed to the Eastern Army's eventual success.

WHERE Sekigahara, Japan.

WHEN October 21, 1600

WHY The death of Toyotomi Hideyoshi, who had acted as unifying figure among the warring Japanese daimyo had plunged the country into a new battle for power.

OUTCOME Ieyasu's victory paved the way for him to become shogun, and establish a dynasty that would endure for over two centuries.

Following a century of civil war in Japan, Toyotomi Hideyoshi had succeeded in unifying the island nation. However, his untimely death in 1598 precipitated a bitter struggle for pre-eminence between former subordinates and led to one of the most decisive battles in Japanese history.

The events of the battle of Sekigakara were considered so momentous in Japanese history that they are commemorated by a stone monument on the site of the conflict.

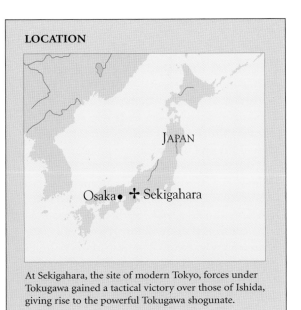

LOCATION

JAPAN

Osaka • ✛ Sekigahara

At Sekigahara, the site of modern Tokyo, forces under Tokugawa gained a tactical victory over those of Ishida, giving rise to the powerful Tokugawa shogunate.

The Battle of Sekigahara pitted the forces of Ishida Mitsunari, loyal to the infant son of Toyotomi Hideyoshi, against those of Tokugawa Ieyasu, daimyo (lord) of the Kanto Plain, who was challenging for the succession.

Ishida had carried out a night-time march on Sekigahara, and was already in position by the time the Eastern Army arrived the next morning and had to deploy in a thick fog. Initial clashes went the Western Army's way, and its opponents faced the prospect of being trapped on three sides. But secret negotiations about defecting had taken place between Tokugawa and several of Ishida's lieutenants, including Kobayakawa Hideaki, who occupied a critical position in the field.

When Ishida signalled for Kobayaka to attack, he was hesitant and eventually joined the battle on the Eastern side. This moment of treachery was observed by several other generals of the Western Army, and they too now switched sides. Eventually, those who remained loyal to Ishida saw the battle was lost and began to march away.

TIMELINE

1500–1000BC	1000–500BC	500BC–0AD	0–500AD	500–1000AD	1000–1500AD	1500–2000AD

Siege of Osaka 1615

KEY FACTS

WHO Tokugawa shogunate led by Tokugawa Ieyasu against Toyotomi Hideyori and his clan.

WHAT Tokugawa Ieyasu made two attempts to attack Toyotomi Hideyori in his stronghold at Osaka and was finally successful in his summer campaign of 1615.

WHERE Osaka, Japan.

WHEN November 1614–January 1615 and May–September 1615

WHY Tokugawa Ieyasu saw Toyotomi Hideyori as a rival and a threat to Japan's internal stability.

OUTCOME After Tokugawa Ieyasu's victory, he was able to eliminate the Toyotomi clan and re-unite Japan under his leadership.

After his great victory at Sekigahara in 1600, Tokugawa Ieyasu had gone on to became Shogun, before passing on the title to his son. He continued to carry real political and military clout, however, and acted forcefully when the Toyotomi clan seemed about to challenge dynastic stability.

SENGOKU PERIOD WARS

TOKUGAWA VICTORY

While the siege of Osaka Castle would be the key to the success of the Tokugawa campaign, a certain amount of fighting in the field would also have taken place between the rival clans.

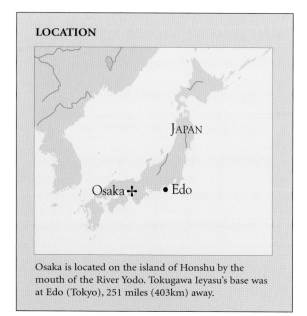

LOCATION

JAPAN

Osaka ✛ • Edo

Osaka is located on the island of Honshu by the mouth of the River Yodo. Tokugawa Ieyasu's base was at Edo (Tokyo), 251 miles (403km) away.

Tokugawa Ieyasu had established himself as Shogun in 1603 after defeating all his enemies at the Battle of Sekigahara in 1600. He stepped down in 1605, nominally handing the shogunate to his son Hidetada. It was a transparent move that fooled few people. Ieyasu would control Japan to the end of his life.

But Ieyasu was concerned about the threat from Toyotomi Hideyori, son and heir of former Japanese ruler Toyotomi Hideyoshi. Hideyori's name was a powerful talisman to many who recalled his father. That made him a threat to the continued domination of the Tokugawa family. Ieyasu, who was 68 and determined to secure the kingdom for his dynasty, decided to deal with the problem now, once and for all.

By the summer of 1614, it was clear that war was going to break out between Ieyasu and Hideyori, with the former gathering all the powder and European-style ordnance he could lay his hands on, including five English cannons. But when the fighting finally broke out, Hideyori decided on a purely defensive strategy, remaining in his

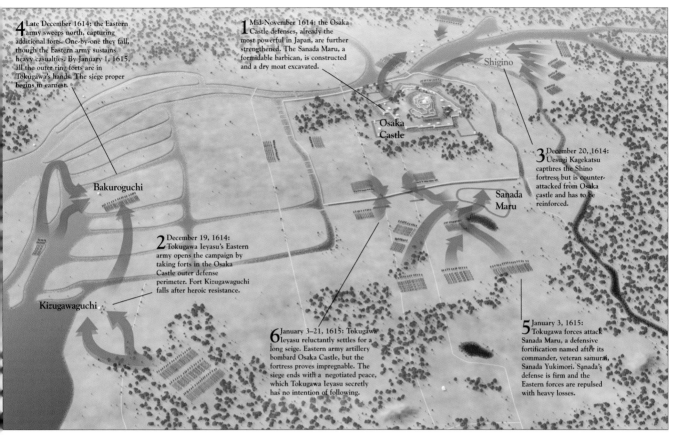

Osaka castle was so well fortified it withstood bombardment by 300 cannons and a painstakingly long and carefully planned siege campaign by the Tokugawa forces. In the end, deceit was required to overcome it.

mighty stronghold of Osaka Castle, passively confident in its powerful defenses. It was hoped that Ieyasu would waste time, men and precious resources trying to take an impregnable fortress.

A LONG SIEGE

Ieyasu launched his Winter Campaign against Osaka in November 1614. By this time, Hideyori had had a massive new moat constructed, 240 feet (73m) wide and 36 feet (11m) deep, and when the waters flowed they rose to a depth of 12–24 feet (3.7–10.4m). The castle fortifications were already formidable and Ieyasu settled for a long siege. 300 cannons were brought up, and these bombarded the castle on a regular basis. Ieyasu ordered one artillery piece to be trained on a tower where he knew Hideyori stayed. One 13lb (6kg) shot smashed through the tower wall and killed two attendants of his mother, Yodogimi.

The castle took some pounding but had been designed well. In fact, as the new moat made it seemingly impregnable, Ieyasu tried trickery. He managed to persuade Yodogimi, who held a position of much

influence over her son, that a truce could be worked out. Foolishly Hideyori agreed, and though most of the Eastern army withdrew, those that remained started to fill in Osaka's moats.

Hideyori protested, but he could make no overt move lest he break the peace agreement. Six months later, Ieyasu resumed the siege, now against defenses rather less formidable than they had been.

BREAKTHROUGH

Ieyasu's troops and cannon could get closer than before, and parts of the castle were blasted to rubble. Soon the main keep was aflame and all hope was lost. Hideyori committed suicide and his mother either killed herself or was dispatched by a retainer. Thousands of Toyotomi loyalists were also put to the sword.

The siege of Osaka marked the end of war and great castle-building. Ieyasu had successfully cemented his shogunate. Peace reigned for over 200 years, until the coming of the Western powers in the mid-1800s began a whole new era for Japan.

TIMELINE

1500–1000BC	1000–500BC	500BC–0AD	0–500AD	500–1000AD	1000–1500AD	1500–2000AD

Siege of Osaka

SIEGE OF OSAKA
Castle siege warfare was essentially a medieval form of battle. In Western Europe, its age had largely passed by the seventeenth century. But Osaka Castle remained a massively strong fortification in China in this period, guarding the mouth of the River Yodo. It was a key stronghold of Toyotomi Hideyori and his clan, as it held out against the Tokugawa shogunate of Tokugawa Ieyasu and his son. Ieyasu pounded the castle with 300 western-style artillery and 300 cannons for months, but still the castle held out. When it finally fell, however, it marked the end of the great age of castle-building.

Breitenfeld 1631

KEY FACTS

WHO King Gustavus Adolphus of Sweden (reigned 1611–1632), and his Saxon allies, against the Imperial army of the Holy Roman Empire under the command of John Tserclaes von Tilly.

WHAT The Imperial forces launched pistol-firing cavalry attacks against their enemy, but the Swedish tactic of interspersing musket units amongst their cavalry, proved a more concentrated form of artillery attack.

WHERE Breitenfeld, north of Leipzig, in modern Germany.

WHEN September 17, 1631

WHY King Gustavus Adolphus was seeking to rally the Protestant cause and to strike at the Hapsburgs' overweening behavior in the Baltic.

OUTCOME After this defeat, Tilly pulled his army back westwards, which was a major boost to the Protestant armies.

During the reign of King Gustavus Adolphus, Sweden soared from being a rather minor Scandinavian power to being a major player on the European stage. Victory at Breitenfeld would be his finest military moment.

THIRTY YEARS' WAR

SWEDISH VICTORY

King Gustavus II Adolphus's success at Breitenfeld owed much to the innovative interspersing of artillery units among the conventional ranks.

LOCATION

SWEDEN

POMERANIA

Breitenfeld ✛ ● Leipzig

FRANCE

● Vienna

Having secured an alliance with the elector of Saxony, King Gustavus Adolphus of Sweden led a Swedish and Saxon army to liberate Leipzig from the Imperialists.

Gustavus Adolphus had declared war on the Imperial Hapsburgs in 1630, and when he finally launched an invasion of Germany the following year, he gained the support of John George, the elector of Saxony, who had just lost the city of Leipzig to an Imperialist army under John Tserclaes von Tilly.

As Gustavus Adolphus and John George moved their armies towards Leipzig, Tilly moved his forces out to meet them and occupied a ridgeline some 5 miles (8km) north of the city, at Breitenfeld. Tilly placed his infantry on the ridgeline, and planned to launch coordinated cavalry attacks against the enemy's flanks, led by his lieutenant, Gottfried Heinrich Graf von Pappenheim on the left, and Tilly himself on the right.

The initial artillery duel favored the Swedes. Not only did they have a greater number of cannon, but, because of their cased ammunition, they delivered a greater volume of fire than the Imperialist artillery. The fire of the Swedish artillery clearly had an effect: the pounding inflicted on Pappenheim's cavalry provoked him to move

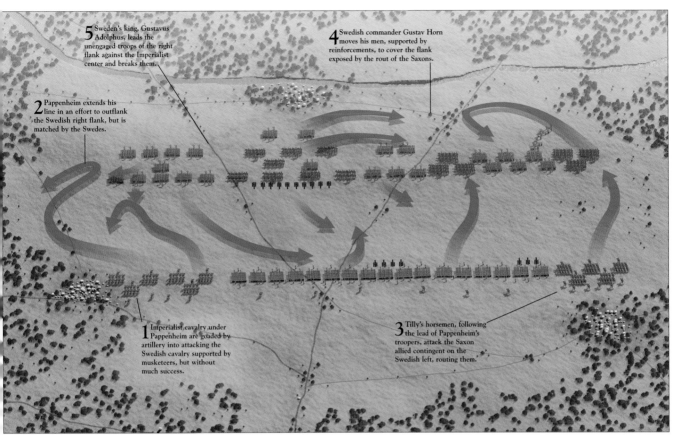

5 Sweden's king, Gustavus Adolphus, leads the unengaged troops of the right flank against the Imperialist center and breaks them.

4 Swedish commander Gustav Horn moves his men, supported by reinforcements, to cover the flank exposed by the rout of the Saxons.

2 Pappenheim extends his line in an effort to outflank the Swedish right flank, but is matched by the Swedes.

1 Imperialist cavalry under Pappenheim are goaded by artillery into attacking the Swedish cavalry supported by musketeers, but without much success.

3 Tilly's horsemen, following the lead of Pappenheim's troopers, attack the Saxon allied contingent on the Swedish left, routing them.

The Imperial army under Tilly enjoyed some success with its own cavalry charges at Breitenfeld, but the Swedish formations were more flexible and their artillery firepower was more effectively concentrated in units.

forwards to avoid the Swedish cannon fire. Because this move was unexpected, Tilly did not order his troops to advance at the same time, and Pappenheim's cavalry therefore advanced without support.

Pappenheim's cavalry attacked the Swedish cavalry, not by charging in and engaging in hand-to-hand combat, but by using the caracole formation. This involved riding up to within pistol range, firing and wheeling to reload and repeat the process. This was a similar concept to countermarch fire for infantry. But it was not effective against the Swedish cavalry because they had intermingled detachments of musketeers among the cavalry units. These inflicted significant casualties on the Imperialist horse because their salvo fire was more densely concentrated and their weapons had both greater range and power of penetration.

On the right flank, things went better for the Imperialists. At the sight of Tilly's cavalry charge, the inexperienced Saxon troops turned on their heels and fled. In a single blow, 40 percent of Gustavus Adolphus's forces had been driven from the field. Fortunately for the

king, his deployment and the discipline of his men did not allow the Imperialist cavalry to roll up his left flank. As fresh Swedes from the reserve and other parts of the battle line arrived, they began pushing the Imperialist forces back with their disciplined volleys.

After about five hours, Pappenheim and his cavalry had finally been driven off. Exhibiting the coup d'oeil of a great captain, Gustavus Adolphus recognized that now was the time to attack. At the head of several troops of horsemen, he led an attack on the Imperialist center, breaking through and capturing Tilly's cannon, which he turned on their former owners. The breaking of their center and the additional artillery pounding was too much for the Imperialists who finally broke. The Swedish cavalry pursued, leaving some 7,600 Imperialist troops dead and another 6,000 as prisoners. The Swedes lost 2,000 men. Breitenfeld had showed the superiority of the "Swedish synthesis" combination of firepower and shock coupled with superior discipline and organizational flexibility. Many larger armies in the following years would copy their example.

TIMELINE

1500–1000BC	1000–500BC	500BC–0AD	0–500AD	500–1000AD	1000–1500AD	1500–2000AD

Lützen 1632

KEY FACTS

WHO A Swedish army, commanded by King Gustavus Adolphus (1594–1632), opposed by an Imperial army under Prince Albrecht von Wallenstein (1583–1634).

WHAT Despite the death of Gustavus Adolphus, the Swedish army was able to win a hard-fought victory.

WHERE Lützen, near Leipzig in Saxony.

WHEN November 6, 1632

WHY Saxony, a Swedish ally, was threatened with invasion by Imperial forces.

OUTCOME Saxony was preserved, but the war continued for another 16 years.

Gustavus Adolphus, King of Sweden, had declared war on the Hapsburg Empire in 1630 and led the first modern-style professional standing army in Europe to a brilliant victory at Breitenfeld. He would at Lützen, too, but at the cost of his own life and high casualties among his troops.

THIRTY YEARS' WAR

SWEDISH VICTORY

King Gustavus Adolphus would lead the Swedish troops on a cavalry charge at Lützen, but this talented and innovative military man would also meet his end in the battle.

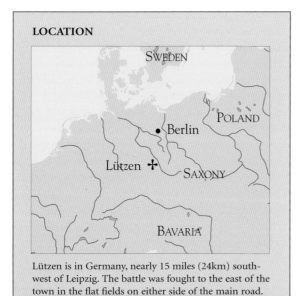

LOCATION

Lützen is in Germany, nearly 15 miles (24km) southwest of Leipzig. The battle was fought to the east of the town in the flat fields on either side of the main road.

Victory at Breitenfeld allowed the Swedes to overrun much of southern Germany in 1631–32 and the Holy Roman Emperor placed the experienced Prince Albrecht von Wallenstein in command of a fightback. After inflicting an early defeat on the Swedish army, Wallenstein marched into Saxony to go into winter quarters, and detached some of his cavalry. But the Swedes were still in the field and seeking a decisive battle before the ravaged winter countryside ran out of supplies to support their campaign.

Joining forces with the Saxons to create an allied army, they camped overnight near Lützen, on a flat plain that had little shelter, with the Imperial army just 3 miles (5km) away.

Thick fog forced the Allied army to postpone its attack until 11:00 a.m. the next day, after which their advance was halted by heavy musket and artillery fire. On the right, a primarily Swedish and Finnish force under the personal command of Gustavus Adolphus made more progress, though at a heavy cost in terms of casualties. Fog then descended on the battlefield once more, heavily

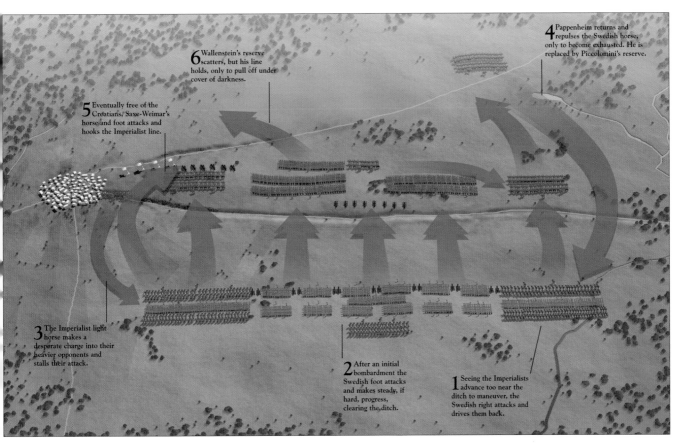

6 Wallenstein's reserve scatters, but his line holds, only to pull off under cover of darkness.

4 Pappenheim returns and repulses the Swedish horse, only to become exhausted. He is replaced by Piccolomini's reserve.

5 Eventually free of the Croatians, Saxe-Weimar's horse and foot attacks and hooks the Imperialist line.

3 The Imperialist light horse makes a desperate charge into their heavier opponents and stalls their attack.

2 After an initial bombardment the Swedish foot attacks and makes steady, if hard, progress, clearing the ditch.

1 Seeing the Imperialists advance too near the ditch to maneuver, the Swedish right attacks and drives them back.

Lützen was fought on a flat plain with little shelter. There was plenty of room for the old favorite of European warfare over the centuries, the cavalry charge, which relied upon speed, maneuver and shock force.

restricting visibility. The result was a close-quarters battle of attrition with heavy casualties on both sides.

In the midst of the fighting, Wallenstein's army were buoyed by the arrival of the detached cavalry—5,000 horsemen under Count Pappenheim (1594–1632)—and the Swedish cavalry were almost driven from the field. Meanwhile, Gustavus Adolphus had taken personal command of one of his cavalry units when its commander was wounded. As he led an advance, the fog thickened until it was impossible to see in any direction. This covered the attack of a force of Imperial cuirassiers, who charged into Gustavus Adolphus's unit.

In the ensuing mêlée, Gustavus Adolphus was shot in the arm and lost his sword as he tried to keep control of his horse. He became separated from his command and was shot again, this time in the back. Despite the efforts of his bodyguard to save him, Gustavus Adolphus fell from his horse when it was shot, and he was dragged for some distance with his foot caught in a stirrup. He was still alive when the Imperial cavalry found him, and was finished off with a pistol shot. His clothing and weapons were taken as trophies.

Recognizing the wounded horse that fled through their lines, and hearing that the king was dead, the Swedes began to waver. However, the army's second-in-command, Bernhard of Saxe-Weimar (1604–39), was able to rally them and lead an advance. A general attack developed that became a bitter close-range firefight.

In a final effort to break the deadlock, Bernhard of Saxe-Weimar ordered an attack on the Imperial artillery battery located on Windmill Hill. Supported by intense artillery fire, the allies were initially repulsed and a second assault succeeded only after two further hours of close combat. With Windmill Hill in the possession of the allies, the Imperial position was badly compromised.

Wallenstein's army was demoralized and exhausted and, although his opponents were in scarcely better condition, it was the Imperial forces that retreated. The allied victory had cost them 3,000 casualties, against 4,000 Imperial losses. Despite this battlefield victory, the overall strategic victory sought by Gustavus Adolphus had eluded him, and whatever advantage was gained at Lützen was bought at the price of his own life.

TIMELINE

1500–1000BC	1000–500BC	500BC–0AD	0–500AD	500–1000AD	1000–1500AD	1500–2000AD

Battle of the Downs 1639

By the 1630s, the formidable naval powers of Spain and England were weakening, but the seas they had so recently dominated were witnessing the rise of a belligerently confident new maritime power in the Dutch.

EIGHTY YEARS' WAR

DUTCH VICTORY

KEY FACTS

WHO The Dutch lieutenant-admiral Maarten Tromp against a Spanish fleet led by Admiral Antonio de Oquendo.

WHAT A belligerent Dutch admiral launched an audacious attack on Spanish ships within neutral English waters.

WHERE The Downs, off the Kent coast, England.

WHEN October 31, 1639

WHY A Spanish fleet was attempting to bring reinforcements to its beleaguered troops in Flanders during the ongoing Eighty Years' War.

OUTCOME The Spanish mission to deliver troop reinforcements did to some extent succeed, but the victory was an emphatic statement of growing confidence of the Dutch as a naval power.

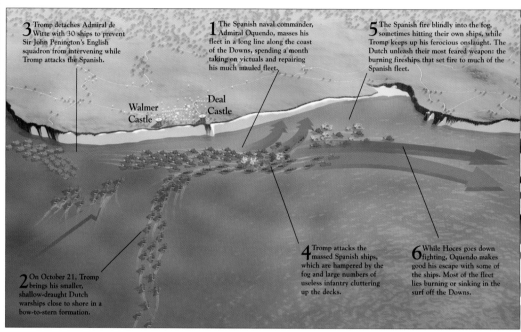

3 Tromp detaches Admiral de Witte with 30 ships to prevent Sir John Penington's English squadron from intervening while Tromp attacks the Spanish.

1 The Spanish naval commander, Admiral Oquendo, masses his fleet in a long line along the coast of the Downs, spending a month taking on victuals and repairing his much mauled fleet.

5 The Spanish fire blindly into the fog, sometimes hitting their own ships, while Tromp keeps up his ferocious onslaught. The Dutch unleash their most feared weapon: the burning fireships that set fire to much of the Spanish fleet.

Walmer Castle

Deal Castle

2 On October 21, Tromp brings his smaller, shallow-draught Dutch warships close to shore in a bow-to-stern formation.

4 Tromp attacks the massed Spanish ships, which are hampered by the fog and large numbers of useless infantry cluttering up the decks.

6 While Hoces goes down fighting, Oquendo makes good his escape with some of the ships. Most of the fleet lies burning or sinking in the surf off the Downs.

The Battle of the Downs took place in the English Channel, in waters not far from two of Britain's most famous coastal fortresses at Walmer and Deal. But on this occasion, the naval protagonists were the Dutch and Spanish fleets.

LOCATION

North Sea

ENGLAND

DUTCH PROVINCES

✛ Downs

FRANCE

The Downs lies on the coast of Kent between Walmer castle and the strategic port of Dover in the southeast of England, facing the Channel and France.

A fleet of Spanish ships had been trying to bring reinforcement troops to its army in Flanders when they were sighted by the Dutch Admiral Maarten Tromp, who launched an attack in the English Channel. The Spanish admiral Antonio de Oquendo, more concerned with delivering the soldiers safely than engaging the Dutch in a sea battle, fled with his ships for the dubious safety of Spain's former enemy, England, taking anchorage at the Downs, on the Kent coast.

After waiting for reinforcements, and realizing that the Spanish would not come out to give battle, Tromp attacked, even though he was in technically neutral English water. Firing quick rounds and coming in close for a kill, his crews trusted in their audacity against an inexperienced enemy. The Spanish ships were raked with shot, and Tromp then unleashed his fireships with devastating results.

The *Santa Theresa*, flagship of Admiral de Hoces, exploded, taking both the admiral and his crew to the seabed. Oquendo managed to escape with the remains of his fleet and delivered some of the promised troops to the Cardinal-Infante's army in Flanders.

TIMELINE

1500–1000BC	1000–500BC	500BC–0AD	0–500AD	500–1000AD	1000–1500AD	1500–2000AD

Edgehill 1642

In the autumn of 1642, as England was about to be consumed by full-scale civil war, Charles I attempted to march on London but found his way blocked by the troops of the Earl of Essex.

KEY FACTS

WHO The Royalist army under Charles I against the Parliamentarians under the Earl of Essex.

WHAT The first major battle of the English Civil War involving the king. After inconclusive artillery salvoes, the two sides engaged in fierce hand-to-hand fighting.

WHERE The escarpment of Edgehill, Warwickshire, England.

WHEN October 23, 1642

WHY Charles I's absolutist conceptions of kingship and his arrest of leading parliamentarians when they refused to support his plans for war with Scotland had split the country in two, precipitating civil war.

OUTCOME After a fierce infantry battle, Charles was unable to dislodge Essex's forces, but was eventually able to move on London.

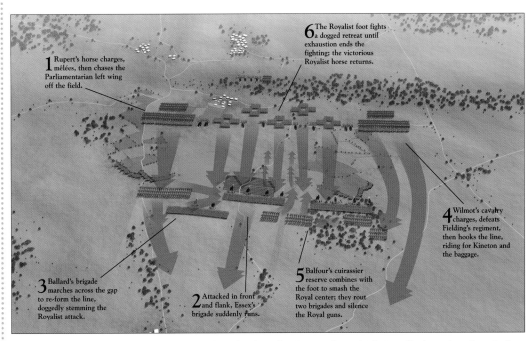

1 Rupert's horse charges, mêlées, then chases the Parliamentarian left wing off the field.

2 Attacked in front and flank, Essex's brigade suddenly runs.

3 Ballard's brigade marches across the gap to re-form the line, doggedly stemming the Royalist attack.

4 Wilmot's cavalry charges, defeats Fielding's regiment, then hooks the line, riding for Kineton and the baggage.

5 Balfour's cuirassier reserve combines with the foot to smash the Royal center; they rout two brigades and silence the Royal guns.

6 The Royalist foot fights a dogged retreat until exhaustion ends the fighting; the victorious Royalist horse returns.

By the time of Edgehill, artillery was a staple of warfare, but often inexpertly used. The Royalist forces here launched rounds of fusilades which, because of poor positioning, simply lodged harmlessly into the turf of the hill.

LOCATION

SCOTLAND

IRELAND

ENGLAND

Edgehill ✛ •London

Edgehill is near Kineton in the English Midlands. The battle was fought on open, boggy moorland. Today much of it is covered by a military depot.

King Charles I had maneuvered his army between the Earl of Essex's Parliamentarians and London, forcing them to offer battle near the foot of Edgehill escarpment, 20 miles (32km) south of Coventry. With both sides deployed, the Royalists chose to attack, first launching their artillery fire. However, they had inexpertly placed their guns up the slope of the hill, so that much of the fire simply plunged uselessly into the turf.

Still, when the royal dragoons on the wings moved forward, they managed to drive back those of their opponents. Following this, Prince Rupert of the Rhine launched a cavalry charge that helped rout the Parliamentarian's central brigade of foot soldiers. However, several other brigades of foot soldiers remained in their ground, and provided enough cover for their cavalry to then break though and punch a hole in the royal lines, breaking up two of their brigades and driving the king's army back to its starting position. Both sides lost around 1,500 men, but while Essex's army was still essentially intact when he withdrew from the field, the way was now effectively clear for the king to march on the capital, London.

TIMELINE

1500–1000BC	1000–500BC	500BC–0AD	0–500AD	500–1000AD	1000–1500AD	1500–2000AD

The Dunes 1658

The English New Model Army broke with tradition in favor of efficiency in combat. At the time, armies were raised on an ad hoc basis and led by political rather than military figures. The New Model Army promoted professionalism and demonstrated a better way to form a military force.

FRANCO-SPANISH WAR

FRENCH & ENGLISH VICTORY

KEY FACTS

WHO French army led by Vicomte de Turenne, supported by troops from the English Commonwealth, against the Spanish army led by John of Austria the Younger and Louis II de Conde.

WHAT A Spanish army was marching to relive Dunkirk, but found itself caught in the rapid volley fire of the English musketeers.

WHERE Dunkirk, modern France.

WHEN June 14, 1658

WHY France was at the time engaged in war with Spain. Meanwhile, the presence of such a large contingent of Spanish troops across the Channel was seen as a potential invasion force by the English.

OUTCOME Defeat of the Spanish at the Dunes ended the treat of an invasion of England, and the Spanish and French would sign a peace treaty the following year.

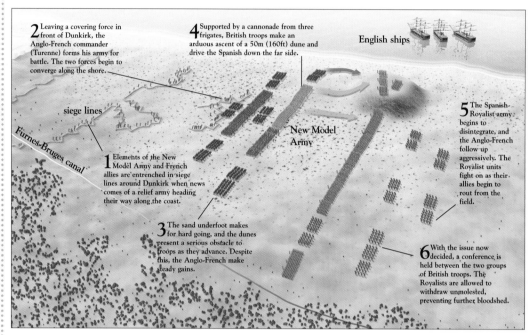

2 Leaving a covering force in front of Dunkirk, the Anglo-French commander (Turenne) forms his army for battle. The two forces begin to converge along the shore.

4 Supported by a cannonade from three frigates, British troops make an arduous ascent of a 50m (160ft) dune and drive the Spanish down the far side.

English ships

siege lines

Furnes-Bruges canal

1 Elements of the New Model Army and French allies are entrenched in siege lines around Dunkirk when news comes of a relief army heading their way along the coast.

New Model Army

5 The Spanish-Royalist army begins to disintegrate, and the Anglo-French follow up aggressively. The Royalist units fight on as their allies begin to rout from the field.

3 The sand underfoot makes for hard going, and the dunes present a serious obstacle to troops as they advance. Despite this, the Anglo-French make steady gains.

6 With the issue now decided, a conference is held between the two groups of British troops. The Royalists are allowed to withdraw unmolested, preventing further bloodshed.

The discipline of the much vaunted New Model Army would be thoroughly tested in the sandy, unstable terrain at the Dunes, when it had to negotiate a steep climb of around 50m (160ft) before it could force its opponents into a retreat.

LOCATION

ENGLAND

DUTCH REPUBLIC

The Dunes ✛

SPANISH NETHERLANDS

• Paris

FRANCE

The region around Dunkirk has been fought over several times throughout history due to its importance as a Channel port.

In 1654, the New Model Army, which had performed so well in the English Civil War, found itself fighting alongside French troops against the Spanish, led by John of Austria the Younger and Louis II de Conde. Dunkirk had been occupied by Spanish troops and when a Spanish relief force marched on the town, the Anglo-French army offered battle on a coastal terrain characterized by many sand dunes.

The musketeers of the English units proved especially effective, maintaining a steady fire by the constant rotation of men. After firing, the front rank retired to the rear to reload while men with weapons ready replaced them and, using forked stands to support their heavy firearms, took aim and fired at the enemy before pulling back in turn. Thus a constant, rolling fire was maintained without exposing the unit to counytercharge, the covering pikemen ready to repulse anyone who got too close.

When an enemy unit was seen to waver, the pikemen advanced to decide the matter with a "push of pike." The Spanish were thrown back on the defensive and sent routing from the field after two hours of hard fighting. Dunkirk itself soon surrendered.

TIMELINE

1500–1000BC	1000–500BC	500BC–0AD	0–500AD	500–1000AD	1000–1500AD	1500–2000AD

Medway 1667

KEY FACTS

WHO — Dutch fleet and marines under the command of Lieutenant Admiral Michiel de Ruyter, against English led by Admiral George Monck, Duke of Albemarle.

WHAT — The Dutch were able to sail up the Thames and the Medway rivers and burn 13 English ships and tow away two others.

WHERE — Chatham, England.

WHEN — June 9–14, 1667

WHY — Charles II had procrastinated over signing a peace treaty to end the Anglo-Dutch War.

OUTCOME — The raid forced the English to come to terms more quickly, agreeing to a treaty that was significantly more favorable to the Dutch.

The English were probably being overly confident when maneuvering behind the scenes for advantageous terms at the conclusion of the Anglo-Dutch War. But an impudent Dutch raid under their noses meant it would be their opponents who left the negotiating table with the biggest smiles.

The ships that sailed from Chatham and the Medway enabled Britain to command seas around the globe for large periods between the sixteenth and nineteenth centuries. The Dutch raid here was a cause of national embarrassment.

LOCATION

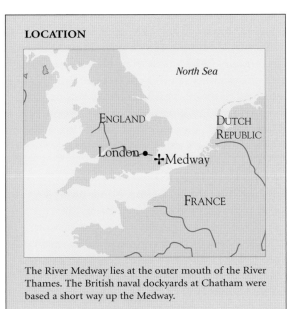

The River Medway lies at the outer mouth of the River Thames. The British naval dockyards at Chatham were based a short way up the Medway.

The Dutch fleet under the command of Admiral de Ruyter reached the mouth of the Thames on June 7 with the intention of raiding up the Medway River and forcing England to sue for peace. Three days later, the Dutch attacked Sheerness, clearing the way for the fleet.

The English responded by placing blocking ships, a chain and two gun batteries at the mouth of the river at Gillingham to keep the enemy away from the main English naval base, at Chatham. The Dutch used fireships to smash their way through the English defenses on June 12, burning several ships in the process and capturing HMS *Royal Charles* intact. The following day, the Dutch sailed further up river, but in the face of increasingly heavy English battery fire progress was slow. Another three English vessels were either sunk or captured before the Dutch withdrew to home waters. The raid was a major military and political success for the Dutch, and a serious humiliation for the English navy. A peace agreement was signed on Dutch terms soon afterwards.

TIMELINE

1500–1000BC	1000–500BC	500BC–0AD	0–500AD	500–1000AD	1000–1500AD	1500–2000AD

Kahlenberg 1683

The grand viziers of the Ottoman Empire had nursed ambitions for greater territorial expansion deep into Europe for some time, and the conquest of the strategically vital city of Vienna lay at the heart of their plans.

GREAT TURKISH WAR

HAPSBURG/ROMAN VICTORY

KEY FACTS

Who An army of the Holy Roman Empire, led by Charles of Lorraine, joined by Jan Sobieski III of Poland, against the Ottoman siege forces of Kara Mustafa.

What The Ottomans laid siege to Vienna, but were weakened by fighting on two fronts – continuing their assault on the city, while trying to beat off the relief army.

Where Vienna, Austria.

When September 11, 1683

Why The Ottomans were intent on taking Vienna as part of ambitions to press further on into central Europe.

Outcome The Ottomans sustained heavy and demoralizing losses, and the defeat effectively ended their expansionist ambitions within Europe.

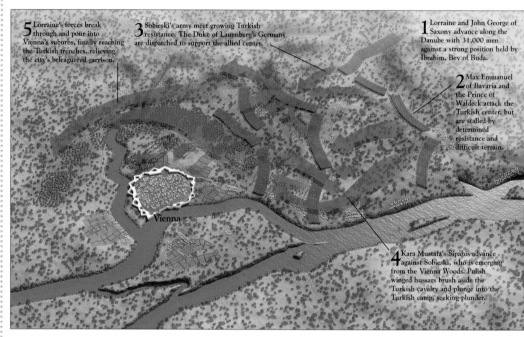

5 Lorraine's forces break through and pour into Vienna's suburbs, finally reaching the Turkish trenches, relieving the city's beleaguered garrison.

3 Sobieski's army meet growing Turkish resistance. The Duke of Lauenberg's Germans are dispatched to support the allied center.

1 Lorraine and John George of Saxony advance along the Danube with 31,000 men against a strong position held by Ibrahim, Bey of Buda.

2 Max Emmanuel of Bavaria and the Prince of Waldeck attack the Turkish center, but are stalled by determined resistance and difficult terrain.

Vienna

4 Kara Mustafa's Sipahis advance against Sobieski, who is emerging from the Vienna Woods. Polish winged hussars brush aside the Turkish cavalry and plunge into the Turkish camp, seeking plunder.

The bravery of the Polish cavalry was renowned for centuries. In 1683, the fabulous "Winged Hussars" swept from the Vienna Woods to lift a prolonged siege by the Turks and end their dreams of conquering Europe.

The Ottoman siege of Vienna had gone on for two months when a relief army of the Holy Roman Emperor, led by Charles of Lorraine, joined by Jan Sobieski III of Poland, arrived on the north bank of the Danube. The Ottoman grand vizier Kara Mustafa was confident Vienna would fall before it could be relieved, and had kept many of his janissaries ready in trenches just outside the walls as sappers continued their attempts to breach them, meaning the attentions of his forces were divided. The combined armies, meanwhile, advanced through the Vienna Woods, sweeping down from the heights of the Kahlenberg mountain.

LOCATION

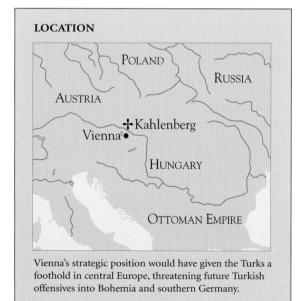

POLAND

RUSSIA

AUSTRIA

✝ Kahlenberg
Vienna ●

HUNGARY

OTTOMAN EMPIRE

Vienna's strategic position would have given the Turks a foothold in central Europe, threatening future Turkish offensives into Bohemia and southern Germany.

WINGED HUSSAR ATTACK

Heavy fighting through the Vienna Woods slowed the advance, but Lorraine broke through along the Danube, and the Poles fought their way through on the right. The "Winged Hussars" of Sobieski's cavalry poured into the Turkish camp in a massive charge. The jannisaries in the trenches were annihilated, and less than three hours after the charge, Vienna had been saved.

TIMELINE

1500–1000BC	1000–500BC	500BC–0AD	0–500AD	500–1000AD	1000–1500AD	1500–2000AD

Ulan Butung 1690

The Chinese Qing army of the seventeenth century was extremely versatile. But when it met the Zungharians at Ulan Butung, having marched across the arid Gobi Desert, its military sophistication was thwarted by a most unconventional "fortification"—a defensive walls of camels.

QING DYNASTY WARS

NO CLEAR VICTORY

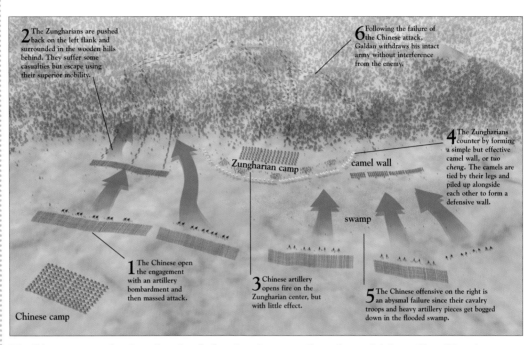

2 The Zungharians are pushed back on the left flank and surrounded in the wooden hills behind. They suffer some casualties but escape using their superior mobility.

6 Following the failure of the Chinese attack, Galdan withdraws his intact army without interference from the enemy.

Zungharian camp

camel wall

4 The Zungharians counter by forming a simple but effective camel wall, or *tuo cheng*. The camels are tied by their legs and piled up alongside each other to form a defensive wall.

swamp

1 The Chinese open the engagement with an artillery bombardment and then massed attack.

Chinese camp

3 Chinese artillery opens fire on the Zungharian center, but with little effect.

5 The Chinese offensive on the right is an abysmal failure since their cavalry troops and heavy artillery pieces get bogged down in the flooded swamp.

The Chinese army was already on the point of exhaustion after many miles on the march in hot, arid conditions, but encountering an unexpectedly effective 'fortification' made from a wall of camels tested their resilience to breaking point.

LOCATION

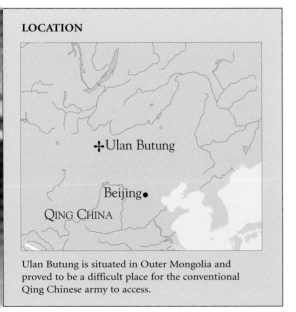

✠ Ulan Butung

Beijing •

QING CHINA

Ulan Butung is situated in Outer Mongolia and proved to be a difficult place for the conventional Qing Chinese army to access.

The Qing forces found Outer Mongolia a challenging battleground. Their supply lines were stretched to a maximum from early in the campaign, and food and water was difficult to manage. Having finally caught up with the Zungharians amidst the wooden hills of Ulan Butung, the Qing employed a combined force of artillery, infantry and cavalry in a traditional combined-arms attack. Caught by surprise, the Zungharian commander, Galdan, decided to stand and fight.

After suffering an artillery bombardment, the Zungharians protected their camp in a highly unconventional fashion, forming a defensive barrier by trussing up their 10,000 camels into a *tuo cheng*, or camel wall, and firing arrows at the Qing through the gaps. Although the Chinese commander Yu claimed a victory when his troops made a breakthrough on the left flank, the main attack proved a failure, which enabled the bulk of the Zungharian cavalry army to survive and withdraw intact after negotiating a cease-fire.

The camel wall proved decisive, in that the Zungharians were able to hold their positions while at their most vulnerable, allowing them to survive to fight another day.

TIMELINE

1500–1000BC	1000–500BC	500BC–0AD	0–500AD	500–1000AD	1000–1500AD	1500–2000AD

Blenheim 1704

KEY FACTS

WHO An Allied force commanded by the Duke of Marlborough (1650–1722) and Prince Eugène of Savoy (1663–1736), opposed by a Franco-Bavarian army under Marshal Count de Tallard (1652–1728).

WHAT The Allies exploited their advantages, notably in infantry and artillery, with bold strategic movement and aggressive tactics on the field of battle.

WHERE The village of Blenheim in Bavaria.

WHEN August 13, 1704

WHY The Grand Alliance sought to limit Franco-Bavarian power by defeating their army in the field.

OUTCOME A decisive victory for the Allies protected Vienna and forced Bavaria out of the war.

Knowing that the fall of Vienna might spell the end of the Grand Alliance, the Duke of Marlborough embarked upon a daring march from the Low Countries to the Danube, putting his forces in position to defeat a Franco-Bavarian army threatening the Austrian capital.

WAR OF THE SPANISH SUCCESSION

ALLIED VICTORY

The battle was characterized by a day of exhausting attacks and counter-attacks which wore down both sides, before Marlborough's English troops eventually gained the day.

LOCATION

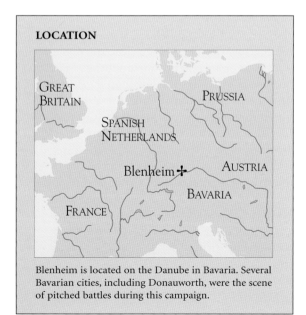

Blenheim is located on the Danube in Bavaria. Several Bavarian cities, including Donauworth, were the scene of pitched battles during this campaign.

France had been generally successful against the Grand Alliance in the War of the Spanish Succession, and with its ally Bavaria now threatening Vienna, there was a danger that Austria, one of the major powers amongst the Allies, could be taken out of the war. John Churchill, later Duke of Marlborough, who was a minister of Queen Anne and an able commander, hit upon a plan to lead an Allied army, currently engaged in the Low Countries, on a daring, rapid march to the Danube to meet the Franco-Bavarian army, commanded by Marshal Count de Tallard.

The Franco-Bavarian army occupied a good defensive position around Blenheim, its right flank secured by the Danube and the left by high, forested, ground. The villages of Blenheim, Oberglau and Lutzingen formed strong points in the line. Low-lying and wet areas formed natural obstacles to any enemy advance. But Marlborough was an aggressive and skilled commander. Wary of Tallard's dispositions, he noted that his personal command on the right flank in front of the village of Blenheim was the strongest part of the Franco-Bavarian line. It seemed likely

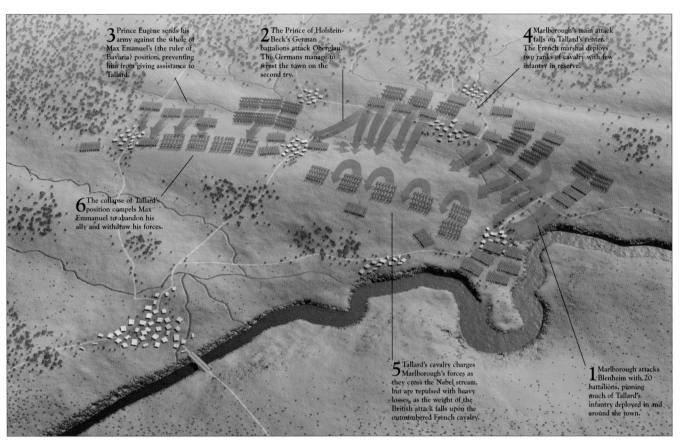

3 Prince Eugène sends his army against the whole of Max Emanuel's (the ruler of Bavaria) position, preventing him from giving assistance to Tallard.

2 The Prince of Holstein-Beck's German battalions attack Oberglau. The Germans manage to wrest the town on the second try.

4 Marlborough's main attack falls on Tallard's center. The French marshal deploys two ranks of cavalry with few infantry in reserve.

6 The collapse of Tallard's position compels Max Emmanuel to abandon his ally and withdraw his forces.

5 Tallard's cavalry charges Marlborough's forces as they cross the Nebel stream, but are repulsed with heavy losses, as the weight of the British attack falls upon the outnumbered French cavalry.

1 Marlborough attacks Blenheim with 20 battalions, pinning much of Tallard's infantry deployed in and around the town.

Blenheim was traditionally depicted in later years as a battle in which cavalry played the main role, whereas it actually featured highly intensive use of artillery, weaponry that was becoming increasingly decisive on the battlefield.

to Marlborough that Tallard intended to counter-attack from here if the opportunity presented itself. Marlborough therefore decided to occupy this force while he broke the weaker center.

Using the army under Prince Eugène of Savoy to occupy the Bavarians holding the enemy left, Marlborough launched the Blenheim pinning attack. The initial attack penetrated Blenheim at a few points, but the Allies were swiftly ejected and were then counter-attacked in the flank by cavalry. Fire from an Allied infantry brigade drove off the counter-attack in turn, allowing a renewed attack to be launched. This drew in French reinforcements, with the result that there were far more men in the village than were necessary to beat off the Allied assault. The attack on Blenheim was an expensive failure, in that it did not drive the French from the village, but it did serve the purpose of pinning large numbers of French troops in a position where they could not influence the critical phase of the battle.

The point of decision was Oberglau, in the center, held by the French under Ferdinand de Marsin. As the Allied

infantry advanced, they were charged by French horsemen, and repulsed by artillery fire. Had Tallard's infantry reserves not been occupied at Blenheim, a French counter-attack at this point might have borne fruit. Instead, additional Allied cavalry, including heavy squadrons sent by Prince Eugène, enabled the French center to be pushed back into the village of Oberglau, were their infantry were overwhelmed despite a gallant stand.

On the Allied right flank, Prince Eugène personally led another attack, the regimental color in his hand, just at the moment when some of his troops seemed to be wavering. This finally broke the Bavarian line. Now only the French right flank force still held out in and around Blenheim, but gradually they were pushed into the center of the village, where they made a stand in a walled churchyard. There, they beat off repeated attacks with heavy casualties on both sides until the Allies offered a parlay. The defenders eventually agreed to surrender, bringing the action to a close. The Grand Alliance remained intact, and Marlborough made a Duke.

TIMELINE

1500–1000BC	1000–500BC	500BC–0AD	0–500AD	500–1000AD	1000–1500AD	1500–2000AD

Ramillies 1706

KEY FACTS

WHO John, Duke of Marlborough leads an Anglo-Dutch army against the French under the Duc de Villeroi.

WHAT In one of the great cavalry engagements, a well-executed "secret" redeployment of some of his cavalry squadrons turned what seemed a fruitless mêlée in Marlborough's favor.

WHERE Ramillies, Belgium.

WHEN May 23, 1706

WHY The French were trying to resist Allied inroads into the Spanish Netherlands.

OUTCOME Marlborough was able to enjoy further military success in the Netherlands and push the French army back beyond the Flemish frontier.

There can seldom have been as great a horse charge as that massed by the French cavalry at Ramillies. Yet the pride of their army, despite immense bravery, were to be cut down by the Anglo-Dutch forces under the Duke of Marlborough, who once again proved his shrewdness on the battlefield.

At the height of the battle, the fighting descended into a furious mêlée, with many soldiers crushed to death and no side seeming to gain an advantage as the combatants swayed back and forth.

LOCATION

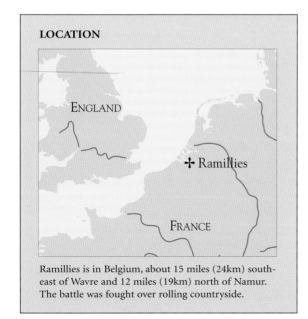

Ramillies is in Belgium, about 15 miles (24km) south-east of Wavre and 12 miles (19km) north of Namur. The battle was fought over rolling countryside.

Louis XIV had ordered Marshal Villeroi to engage the Duke of Marlborough's Anglo-Dutch army after it had penetrated defensive fortifications in the Spanish Netherlands during the ongoing War of the Spanish Succession.

The two armies engaged near the village of Ramillies on broad, rolling, open country, an almost natural arena unbroken by obstacles and bounded by the village of Ramillies to the north and Taviers to the south. It was Villeroi who had a grand cavalry plan. His massive cavalry arm was to sweep forwards and soften up the numerically inferior Allies. They would then follow on with the sword and drive English cavalry on the left from the field. English cavalry, on the allied right, would not have room nor time to deal with the envelopment. Then the horse would have their day, cutting them down and turning the retreat into a spectacular rout. A fitting revenge for Blenheim, but the plan didn't quite work out.

Marlborough's own cavalry option had a chance if something if something could be done to equalize the

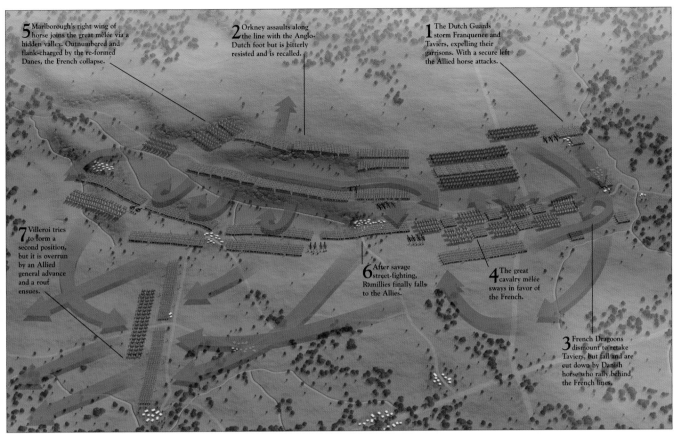

5 Marlborough's right wing of horse joins the great mêlée via a hidden valley. Outnumbered and flank-charged by the re-formed Danes, the French collapse.

2 Orkney assaults along the line with the Anglo-Dutch foot but is bitterly resisted and is recalled.

1 The Dutch Guards storm Franquenee and Taviers, expelling their garrisons. With a secure left the Allied horse attacks.

7 Villeroi tries to form a second position, but it is overrun by an Allied general advance and a rout ensues.

6 After savage street-fighting, Ramillies finally falls to the Allies.

4 The great cavalry mêlée sways in favor of the French.

3 French Dragoons dismount to retake Taviers, but fail and are cut down by Danish horse who rally behind the French lines.

The battle of Ramilles took place in wide open country near the village of Ramillies itself. It was almost a natural arena for warfare – ideal, so it seemed, for the sweeping cavalry charge to be the decisive instrument.

numbers. This meant switching Henry Lumley's cavalry from the right to the left, where their numbers and surprise appearance would make a significant difference. This hinged upon the French not knowing that Lumley was coming. Marlborough sent word to Lumley for the majority of his cavalry to wheel sharply to their left and move off unseen down the shallow Quivelette valley towards the center. It was a calculated risk and it took some time to effect, but when the first 18 squadrons of Lumley's command arrived, Marlborough had enough horsemen to risk undertaking a mêlée en masse with the best cavalry in Europe.

The battle began with a charge of the much admired French cavalry. With 68 squadrons, a cavalry charge on such a scale had seldom been seen before. Literally thousands of horsemen walked and then slow-trotted forwards, boot to boot. This was no furious charge, but a steady steamroller of an advance. What followed was a furious mêlée, with the two sides crashing into one another at the recommended good round trot, spilling men from the saddle and knocking horses over and

sideways in the crush. Both sides' reserves cannoned into the rear of their own formations and sent shockwaves of impetus through the densely packed mass, which swayed back and forth, neither side gaining a clear advantage.

BREAKTHROUGH

The moment of breakthrough came late in the day when Marlborough, placing himself at the head of the 18 newly arrived cavalry squadrons, led them into the battle. It was now a matter of time and attrition. The Allies were winning the cavalry struggle, with a numerical superiority of 87 to 68 squadrons. They drove the French back and then opened up their guns on them. The French Household cavalry had done their best and lived up to their fame, but after nearly two hours of charging and counter-charging, they were finally being overwhelmed. The Allied horse pinned them frontally and surged through the gaps to surround and annihilate them. For the French, it was a final, crushing end to a hard-fought battle; for the Allies, it was a decisive victory.

TIMELINE

1500–1000BC	1000–500BC	500BC–0AD	0–500AD	500–1000AD	1000–1500AD	1500–2000AD

Ramillies

RAMILLIES

Two hundred years after the defeat of Francis I at Pavia by the Hapsburg guns, the French army, under Francois Villeroi's command at Ramillies, remained wedded to the idea of marching infantry and the "glorious" cavalry charge. To be fair, the French were still the finest cavalry in Europe, but now they were taking on a shrewd opponent in John Churchill, Duke of Marlborough, who had already secured his reputation with a brilliant victory at Blenheim the year before. Two hours of French charges and counter charges brought only "the most shameful, disastrous and humiliating of routs."

Oudenarde 1708

KEY FACTS

WHO   John Churchill, Duke of Marlborough and Eugène, Prince of Savoy and the Allied army, against the French under Joseph, Duke of Vendome and Louis, Duke of Burgundy.

WHAT   The French army was undermined by poor communication, mutual distrust and the different objectives of their commanders, in contrast to Marlborough's swift and efficient deployments and communication networks.

WHERE   Oudenarde, modern Belgium.

WHEN   July 11, 1708

WHY   The French had made another attempt to retake the Spanish Netherlands and seemed poised to cut off the British army's supply lines from the English Channel.

OUTCOME Defeat was followed by peace negotiations, but Louis XIV would soon return to his attempt to regain the Netherlands.

In contrast to the neat battle formation, and rampaging cavalry charges at Ramillies, the battle between the Allied army and the French at Oudenarde was just a mad, bloody scramble. But it produced the same outcome—a defeat for the French.

WAR OF THE SPANISH SUCCESSION

ANGLO-DUTCH VICTORY

Keeping supply lines open was key for any army on campaign overseas. Oudenarde was a vital fortress if the British were to retain their lines to the English Channel in the War of Spanish Succession.

LOCATION

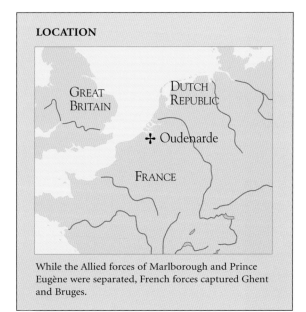

While the Allied forces of Marlborough and Prince Eugène were separated, French forces captured Ghent and Bruges.

Despite several major battles, such as at Blenheim (1704) and Ramillies (1706), the Spanish War of Succession dragged on. The fighting in the Low Countries had reached stalemate until, in 1708, Louis XIV sent a large army under the joint command of the seasoned old soldier the Duke of Vendôme and his grandson and heir, Louis, the Duke of Burgundy.

As the French army prepared for an invasion of Flanders, the Duke of Marlborough, now seemingly outnumbered, was joined by the Imperial army under Prince Eugène of Savoy. When the French persuaded the citizens of Ghent and Bruges in northern Flanders to turn themselves over, thus cutting Marlborough's lines of supply, the Allies, realizing their fortress at Oudenarde was their only remaining link with the English Channel, decided the best option was to engage the French as swiftly as possible.

An Allied advanced guard under quartermaster general William Cadogan secured Oudenarde before the French under Vendôme could reach it. While the latter was

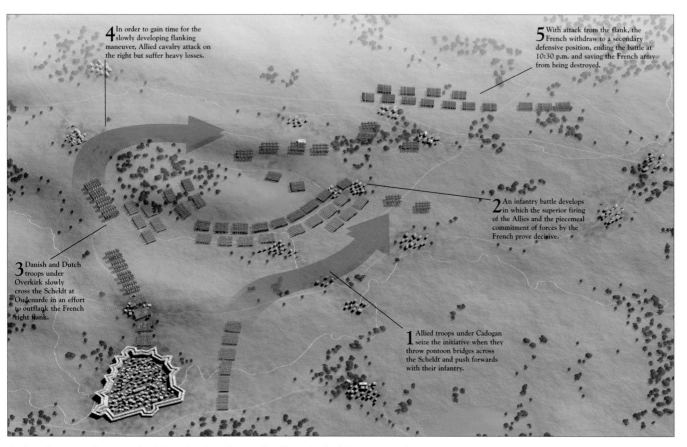

4 In order to gain time for the slowly developing flanking maneuver, Allied cavalry attack on the right but suffer heavy losses.

5 With attack from the flank, the French withdraw to a secondary defensive position, ending the battle at 10:30 p.m. and saving the French army from being destroyed.

2 An infantry battle develops in which the superior firing of the Allies and the piecemeal commitment of forces by the French prove decisive.

3 Danish and Dutch troops under Overkirk slowly cross the Scheldt at Oudenarde in an effort to outflank the French right flank.

1 Allied troops under Cadogan seize the initiative when they throw pontoon bridges across the Scheldt and push forwards with their infantry.

Oudenarde was another example of the Duke of Marlborough's effective leadership. By moving his troops across terrain at a rapid pace while the enemy seemed to be dawdling, he enabled the British to assume the advantageous position, despite being outnumbered.

determined to launch an assault on it, he found to his frustration that he was undermined by Burgundy, who argued for adopting a more defensive position along the River Scheldt. Cadogan spotted that Vendôme's forces were moving at only a leisurely pace to redeploy across the river, and sent word back to Marlborough to arrive as quickly as possible, setting up pontoon bridges across the Scheldt to aid him. Marlborough marched at lightning speed, and this audacious crossing by Allied troops had given them the initiative, even though the French had a considerable numerical advantage.

As the battle began, Burgundy ordered six battalions of French infantry towards the village of Groenewald, but the attack got bogged down. Seeing this, Vendôme ordered another six battalions in support and finally led an additional 12 battalions himself. Eventually Vendôme had committed 50 battalions to the attack against the Allies, but was unable to exercise effective command since he was personally engaged in the infantry battle. Unfortunately, Burgundy seemed unaware of what was happening and did little to support the main attack. He sent 16 cavalry

squadrons, but their advance was halted by the marshy ground. The battle raged on and the superior platoon fire of the allies took its toll.

On the Allied side of the field, the coordination between Marlborough, who was now commanding the Allied left, and Eugène, Prince of Savoy, was exemplary by contrast. Then critical reinforcements arrived in the form of Count Overkirk and his 24 battalions and 12 squadrons of Dutch and Danish troops. Although the battle raged on for some time longer, the arrival of the Dutch and Danes under Overkirk convinced Burgundy that all was lost and he and his entourage left the field. Vendôme held on a bit longer, but was eventually forced to withdraw, joining Burgundy on the road back to Ghent.

Had Overkirk arrived earlier, the entire French army might have been destroyed. As it was, 5,500 French were killed or wounded and another 9,000 captured, including some 800 officers. The Allies also took more than 100 standards and colors and 4,500 horses and mules, losing just under 3,000 killed and wounded from their own strength.

TIMELINE

1500–1000BC	1000–500BC	500BC–0AD	0–500AD	500–1000AD	1000–1500AD	1500–2000AD

Poltava 1709

KEY FACTS

WHO Charles XII of Sweden lead his army against the Russian tsar Peter the Great.

WHAT A Swedish army seriously weakened by a march through the Russian winter, was picked off by a newly efficient Russian artillery power outside Poltava.

WHERE Poltava, Ukraine.

WHEN June 27, 1709

WHY The Swedish had endeavored to continue their military dominance of the region by invading Russia.

OUTCOME Swedish military capability had been critically dented, while Russia announced its arrival as a military force.

Sweden was a relatively small European nation that had punched above its weight for years. The Russians, by contrast, had lagged behind. But once Peter the Great finally mobilized his country's potential military capability, the results could be devastating, as demonstrated at Poltava.

GREAT NORTHERN WAR

RUSSIAN VICTORY

The Swedes had to pass through a narrow area of ground flanked by marshes on one side and woods on the other to confront the Russians at Poltava, and their slim front left them an easy target for Peter the Great's waiting artillery.

LOCATION

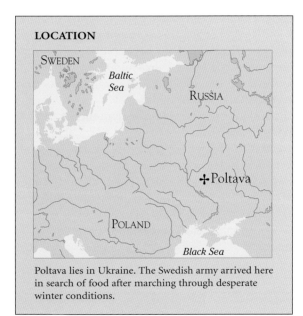

Poltava lies in Ukraine. The Swedish army arrived here in search of food after marching through desperate winter conditions.

Poltava marked the arrival of Russia as a military power, but to do so, it first had to defeat the Swedes, who had been in the ascendency for some time. Charles XII, king of Sweden, had continued his nation's domination of the Scandinavian and Baltic region, established by King Gustavus Adolphus earlier in the previous century, but Russia was increasingly impatient to assert its own presence. While the Swedes were absorbed with attacking Denmark and Poland, the Russian army underwent major reform under the tsar, Peter the Great. When Charles invaded Russia in 1708, it was finally able to put out an army that was fully equipped to meet him.

Charles had made the mistake of invading during a Russian winter, meaning that by the time the main armies encountered one another, what had been a 40,000-strong Swedish force was down to around 22,000 men, whittled away by the cold, sickness and failing supplies, and by being picked off in skirmishes with the Russians. En route to Moscow, instead of waiting for troop reinforcements, Charles decided to lay

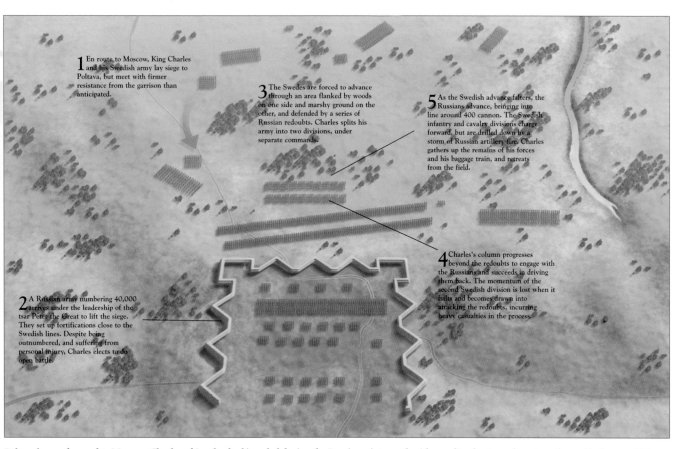

1 En route to Moscow, King Charles and his Swedish army lay siege to Poltava, but meet with firmer resistance from the garrison than anticipated.

2 A Russian army numbering 40,000 arrives under the leadership of the tsar Peter the Great to lift the siege. They set up fortifications close to the Swedish lines. Despite being outnumbered, and suffering from personal injury, Charles elects to do open battle.

3 The Swedes are forced to advance through an area flanked by woods on one side and marshy ground on the other, and defended by a series of Russian redoubts. Charles splits his army into two divisions, under separate commands.

4 Charles's column progresses beyond the redoubts to engage with the Russians and succeeds in driving them back. The momentum of the second Swedish division is lost when it halts and becomes drawn into attacking the redoubts, incurring heavy casualties in the process.

5 As the Swedish advance falters, the Russians advance, bringing into line around 400 cannon. The Swedish infantry and cavalry divisions charge forward, but are drilled down by a storm of Russian artillery fire. Charles gathers up the remains of his forces and his baggage train, and retreats from the field.

Poltava lay on the road to Moscow. Charles of Sweden had invaded during the Russian winter and, with supplies short, was keen to make rapid advances. This would inform his keenness to engage with better-positioned opponents at Poltava.

siege to Poltava, but the garrison within held out longer than anticipated. To add to the problem of dwindling food supplies, gunpowder was also running low.

It was at this moment that a 40,000-strong Russian army arrived under the command of tsar Peter. To make his situation worse, Charles's ability to command was hampered by an infected foot wound, which left him lame.

The sensible move at this point would have been for Charles to draw back as quickly as possible. However, he decided to remain and fight the Russians. The latter had set up fortifications close to the Swedish army, expecting that Charles would aim for a swift resolution of the situation, given his supply issues. They were correct. A Swedish advance meant they had to pass through an area that was flanked by woods on one side and marshy ground on the other. This area was defended by a series of Russian redoubts. Passing the redoubts required splitting the army into two divisions, only one of which could be under Charles's command as he was carried along on a litter.

Unfortunately, Charles was a "lead from the front" leader who did not find it easy to delegate or communicate ideas to subordinates readily. While Charles's column swept beyond the redoubts to engage and drive back the Russians, the second division, confused about its purpose, paused to attack the redoubts, incurring heavy casualties in the process. With this loss of momentum from the Swedish advance, Peter now bought his own 40,000-strong force forward, together with something in the region of 400 cannon.

TORN TO SHREDS

Once again, wisdom might have dictated a sharp withdrawal, but Charles had, from past military experience, developed contempt for the ability of the Russian soldier to hold his ground. So he launched some 4,000 infantry and cavalry on a 660-yard (600m) advance into a storm of Russian artillery fire. Inevitably, the Swedes were torn to shreds. The Swedes had met with savage defeat. In a single battle, the baton of Northern European super power had passed from them to Russia.

TIMELINE

1500–1000BC	1000–500BC	500BC–0AD	0–500AD	500–1000AD	1000–1500AD	1500–2000AD

Poltava

POLTAVA

With all the resources at its disposal, Russia had been punching below its weight for too long on the battlefield, something that Peter the Great was keen to rectify. Fascinated by technology, he invested huge sums in building up his army's artillery firepower. This was unleashed on the Swedes—until then, the mightier fighting force—at Poltava to devastating effect. The battle announced the arrival of Russia as a force to be contended with, and for only one year of Peter's reign the country would not be at war.

Siege of Fredriksten 1718

KEY FACTS

WHO King Charles XII of Sweden against the Norwegian garrison of the town of Fredriksten.

WHAT Frediksten was a key fortress and Charles XII intended to capture it to ensure his army would not be attacked from the rear.

WHERE Fredriksten, near Halden, Norway.

WHEN December 12, 1718

WHY Charles XII was involved in an ongoing battle to capture Denmark-Norway.

OUTCOME Charles XII was killed while making a trench inspection, and the invasion was abandoned.

King Charles XII of Sweden was a fascinating figure and an able military commander. But leading the army in person at the siege of Fredriksten he was mortally injured by a projectile while inspecting the trenches. His death ended Sweden's hopes of conquering neighboring Norway.

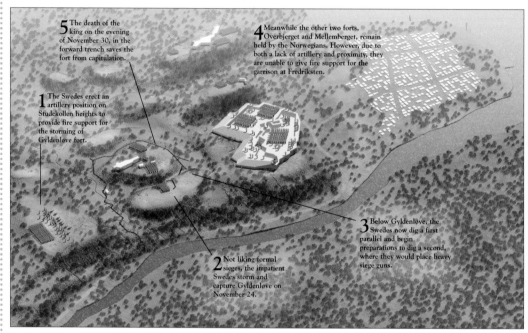

5 The death of the king on the evening of November 30, in the forward trench saves the fort from capitulation.

4 Meanwhile the other two forts, Overbjerget and Mellemberget, remain held by the Norwegians. However, due to both a lack of artillery and proximity, they are unable to give fire support for the garrison at Fredriksten.

1 The Swedes erect an artillery position on Studekollen heights to provide fire support for the storming of Gyldenløve fort.

3 Below Gyldenløve, the Swedes now dig a first parallel and begin preparations to dig a second, where they would place heavy siege guns.

2 Not liking formal sieges, the impatient Swedes storm and capture Gyldenløve on November 24.

Charles XII organized what had seemed likely to be a fruitful siege, but his death while inspecting troops led to its abandonment—and the loss of one of Europe's most accomplished military rulers.

LOCATION

Fredriksten was the key fortress along the frontier with Sweden and located just next to the border town of Fredrikshald in southeastern Norway.

In October 1718, Swedish king Charles XII invaded southern Norway with 35,000 troops, determined to reduce the lynchpin of the enemy's frontier defenses at Fredrikshald to rubble through a regular siege, led by a hired professional French artillery officer called Colonel Maigret.

The Swedes, commanded in person by the king, stormed and captured the outer fort of Gyldenløve on November 24. Three days later, the Swedes, facing only 1,400 enemy troops holding the fortress of Fredriksten, dug a parallel trench to the fortress, followed by an approach trench (to a second parallel), and seemed to be on the verge of a great—and relatively easy—victory.

CHARLES XII'S DEMISE

Once the siege artillery had the fortress within range, it could be forced through bombardment to capitulate, as Colonel Maigret had assured the king. But on November 30 Charles XII was killed in the most mysterious of circumstances in the forward trenches, saving the Norwegians from what would have been a humiliating defeat and eventual occupation by their neighbors.

TIMELINE

1500–1000BC	1000–500BC	500BC–0AD	0–500AD	500–1000AD	1000–1500AD	1500–2000AD

Leuthen 1757

When Frederick the Great led the Prussians at Leuthen in 1757, his reputation as a brilliant general was already secure after his devastating win over the French at Rossbach. After Leuthen, he would earn a place among the greats of legend.

SEVEN YEARS' WAR

PRUSSIAN VICTORY

KEY FACTS

WHO Frederick the Great headed a Prussian army against the Austrians under the command of Charles of Lorraine and Field Marshal Leopold.

WHAT Frederick performed a brilliantly executed, rapid redeployment of his men on the battlefield, which threw his opponents into confusion. Despite their superior numbers, they were unable to recover.

WHERE Leuthen, in modern-day Poland.

WHEN December 5, 1757

WHY The Austrians had retaken Silesia during the ongoing Seven Years' War and Frederick was determined to win it back.

OUTCOME This was Frederick the Great's finest hour, establishing his reputation as a great general for all time and ensuring Prussian control of Silesia.

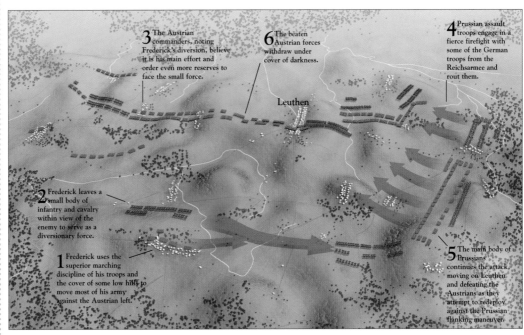

3 The Austrian commanders, noting Frederick's diversion, believe it is his main effort and order even more reserves to face the small force.

6 The beaten Austrian forces withdraw under cover of darkness.

4 Prussian assault troops engage in a fierce firefight with some of the German troops from the Reichsarmee and rout them.

Leuthen

2 Frederick leaves a small body of infantry and cavalry within view of the enemy to serve as a diversionary force.

1 Frederick uses the superior marching discipline of his troops and the cover of some low hills to move most of his army against the Austrian left.

5 The main body of Prussians continues the attack, moving on Leuthen and defeating the Austrians as they attempt to redeploy against the Prussian flanking maneuver.

Frederick the Great's maneuver at Leuthen was skilfully executed. It required much discipline on the part of his soldiers and the ability to cover the terrain quickly, having left only a small body of infantry and cavalry to divert the Austrians.

LOCATION

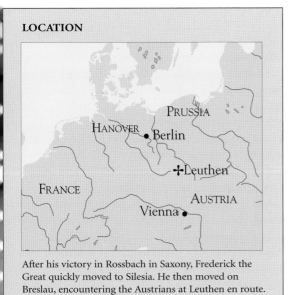

After his victory in Rossbach in Saxony, Frederick the Great quickly moved to Silesia. He then moved on Breslau, encountering the Austrians at Leuthen en route.

Frederick the Great and his Prussian army met the Austrians at Leuthen under the command of Charles of Lorraine and Field Marshal Leopold Daun while marching on the city of Breslau. Frederick took advantage of the excellent discipline and mobility of his troops, as well as the terrain, to undertake a daring and complex maneuver. Using speed and the cover of some low ridges, Frederick marched his army across the front of the Austrian forces and appeared on the Austrian left flank.

EXPOSED FLANK

A small body of infantry and cavalry were left in sight of the Austrians to keep their attention and give the impression he had deployed his army to their front. Frederick quickly attacked the enemy's exposed flank and routed the Reichsarmee units on the far left. The Austrians made an effort to create a new defensive line based on the village of Leuthen, but their slow maneuvering forced units to attack piecemeal, and so the Austrians were driven out of the town and pushed back. Frederick pursued them, but the arrival of night precluded an utter rout in a battle that had lasted for only three hours.

TIMELINE

1500–1000BC	1000–500BC	500BC–0AD	0–500AD	500–1000AD	1000–1500AD	1500–2000AD

Rossbach 1757

KEY FACTS

WHO Frederick the Great of Prussia against the combined armies of France and Austria under Charles de Rohan, Prince de Soubise and General Joseph von Saxe–Hildburghausen.

WHAT With skillful planning, adept use of the terrain and an ability to respond decisively to a changing situation, Frederick the Great brought off a stunning victory.

WHERE Near the village of Rossbach, Saxony, Germany.

WHEN November 5, 1757

WHY Frederick the Great was facing invasion on several fronts and determined to deal with the Franco-Austrian threat first.

OUTCOME Frederick's victory re-invigorated him after earlier reverses and he was now able to deal with the further threats to his realm.

Frederick II of Germany was not given the epithet "the Great" lightly. As a military leader, he was considered a tactical genius, and his brilliance was seldom more evident than at Rossbach.

Frederick the Great was determined to establish Prussia as a European power, which inevitably meant confrontation with two old adversaries, France and Austria.

LOCATION

Frederick chose Saxony as the place to rest his army after the retreat from Bohemia because it offered him a central position in Germany to react to his enemy.

In 1757 Frederick the Great faced the enmity of Austria, and counted Russia and France among his other enemies. The Prussian kingdom lacked the men and money that his opponents could muster. England sided with the soldier-king, but its commitments were largely focused in Hanover and north Germany. Still, the year had begun well enough. Frederick's occupation of Saxony the previous year allowed him to invade Bohemia in the spring. The first months of the campaign found him before the gates of Prague, yet by summer the tide of war had turned. In May an Austrian relief army under Marshal Browne approached the Bohemian capital. With few troops to spare, Frederick marched to meet Browne and defeated him after a bloody day's combat.

A month later the Battle of Kolin was another desperate affair, in which Frederick himself narrowly escaped capture. After suffering 14,000 casualties, Frederick left the field of battle to his enemy, raised the siege of Prague and limped back to Saxony. The situation worsened. France entered the war in the spring of 1757, soon to be joined by

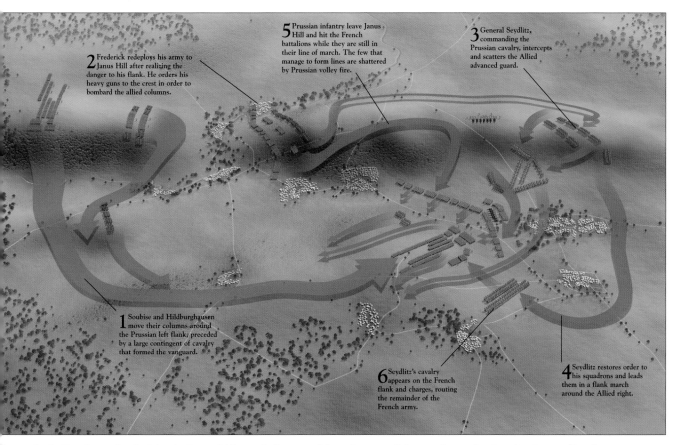

2 Frederick redeploys his army to Janus Hill after realizing the danger to his flank. He orders his heavy guns to the crest in order to bombard the allied columns.

5 Prussian infantry leave Janus Hill and hit the French battalions while they are still in their line of march. The few that manage to form lines are shattered by Prussian volley fire.

3 General Seydlitz, commanding the Prussian cavalry, intercepts and scatters the Allied advanced guard.

1 Soubise and Hildburghausen move their columns around the Prussian left flank, preceded by a large contingent of cavalry that formed the vanguard.

6 Seydlitz's cavalry appears on the French flank and charges, routing the remainder of the French army.

4 Seydlitz restores order to his squadrons and leads them in a flank march around the Allied right.

Success for the Prussians at Rossbach involved an ambitious redeployment of the entire army, all the more impressive given that the complicated movement was completed within just 90 minutes.

Sweden and Russia, and all were ready to hone in on Berlin.

Frederick determined to deal with the Franco-Austrian threat first, whilst the Russian army was too distant to intervene, even though his army would be outnumbered by two to one. The battle of Rossbach, therefore, where he faced a French army under Charles de Rohan, Prince de Soubise, and General Joseph von Saxe-Hildburghausen commanding the Reicharmee, was a deliberate engagement designed to eliminate a strategic threat.

As preparations were made for battle, Hilburghausen and Soubise, instead of advancing head-on, decided they would screen their camp, and move their columns around the Prussian left flank, catching Frederick unawares. It was a sound plan, but it took most of the morning for the French and Imperialists to organize into three march columns.

Frederick, eventually alert to the situation, ordered General von Seydlitz, his cavalry commander, to take all the cavalry and head off the Allied advance, while the Prussian infantry began to march. Taking advantage of a hill to his rear, he ordered his heavy guns to the crest and proceeded to bombard the French from more than a mile off.

Within 90 minutes, Frederick's entire army had redeployed. When Seydlitz unleashed his 38 cavalry squadrons, the surprised Austrian cavalry were hardly able to respond and were sent into flight. As the Prussian infantry moved down the slope towards the French, the Allies were unable to observe their progress due to a dip between their position and the Prussian army. As they emerged, disciplined volleys poured into the head of the Allied columns.

The French battalions faltered. Now Seydlitz's cavalry re-emerged on the French right. The charge of Prussian heavy squadrons took apart the already shaken army. Whatever control Soubise had, disappeared in moments. Another Seydlitz cavalry charge soon put the Imperialists to flight.

Frederick had not only won the day, but the victory transformed the strategic situation that had depressed the Prussian king through the summer. The battle cost Frederick 500 men. For the French and Imperialists, it was much more expensive: 5,000 killed and wounded and another 5,000 captured.

TIMELINE

1500–1000BC	1000–500BC	500BC–0AD	0–500AD	500–1000AD	1000–1500AD	1500–2000AD

Minden 1757

KEY FACTS

WHO   An Anglo-German army led by Field Marshal Ferdinand, Duke of Brunswick, against a French army led by the Marquis de Contades.

WHAT   Massed cavalry charges by the French proved ineffective against the firepower of vastly outnumbered but disciplined use of musketry.

WHERE   Minden, Minden-Ravensburg, now part of North Rhine-Westphalia, Germany.

WHEN   August 1, 1757

WHY   The French were threatening to take control of Hanover in the Seven Years' War.

OUTCOME   After the defeat the French army withdrew from Hanover, while the victory was greeted with great jubilation in Britain.

This was the age of the great cavalry charge, and there was no greater advocate of the cavalryman than Frederick the Great of Prussia. Ironically, however, victory for his Allied Army at Minden would be secured by infantry firepower against the glorious, massed French cavalry.

Minden would feature some of the most dramatic examples of massed cavalry charges, as waves of brave French horsemen launched themselves at the Allied guns. The mounted troops were simply blown to shreds.

LOCATION

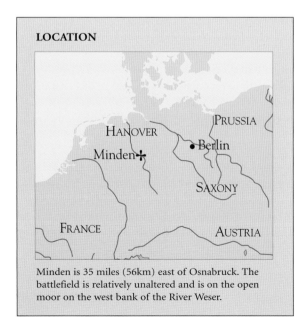

Minden is 35 miles (56km) east of Osnabruck. The battlefield is relatively unaltered and is on the open moor on the west bank of the River Weser.

When the French took control of the strategically vital fortress at Minden on the River Weser in Westphalia, Frederick the Great of Prussia was concerned that Hanover might fall into the hands of his enemy. Prince Ferdinand of Brunswick, charged with maneuvering to deny the French the opportunity of making any further advancement, offered battle to the French under the Marshal, the Marquis de Contades on the plain of Minden.

VAINGLORIOUS CHARGE

The Duke of Marlborough's decisive battles at Blenheim and Ramillies, and the roles played in them by the Allied cavalry, had caught the imagination of public and military men alike. They sent out a signal for the return to shock-mêlée emphasis. Linked to the employment of cavalry "en masse," Minden was to feature a classic example of the spectacular but utterly vainglorious charge.

The most extraordinary moment came when a misunderstood order—the result of linguistic confusion—set off the advance of an Allied column of attack

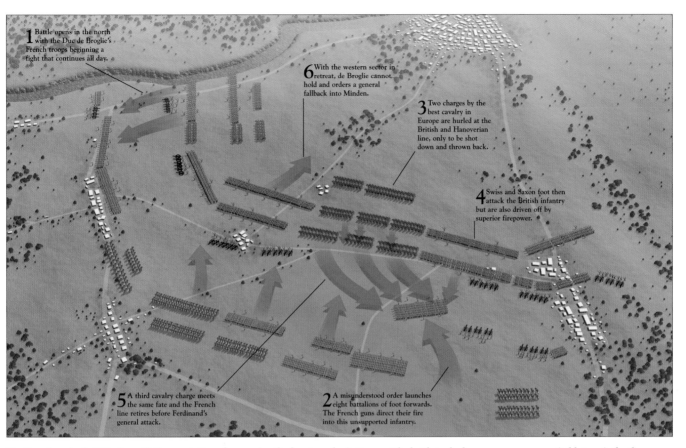

1 Battle opens in the north with the Duc de Broglie's French troops beginning a fight that continues all day.

6 With the western sector in retreat, de Broglie cannot hold and orders a general fallback into Minden.

3 Two charges by the best cavalry in Europe are hurled at the British and Hanoverian line, only to be shot down and thrown back.

4 Swiss and Saxon foot then attack the British infantry but are also driven off by superior firepower.

5 A third cavalry charge meets the same fate and the French line retires before Ferdinand's general attack.

2 A misunderstood order launches eight battalions of foot forwards. The French guns direct their fire into this unsupported infantry.

The French arrived at Minden with the reputation of possessing the finest cavalry in Europe. The battle took place on open moor—suitable terrain for the massed charge of horses—but the cavalry simply crashed into a wall of artillery fire.

commanded by Friedrich von Sporcken and containing six battalions of British infantry, unsupported by cavalry. As they marched, the morning mist lifted to reveal that they were heading directly towards the center of the French line, where stood the elite French cavalry.

While Ferdinand tried to halt the advance, the redcoat line continued to move forward under heavy fire from two batteries of artillery, with the still fresh French cavalrymen licking their lips behind them. When they launched themselves in a mighty wave at the infantry, their combined squadrons amounted to something like 7,500 men. But now the Allied infantry halted and presented muskets. Their first volley crashed into the front rank of the cavalry, bringing down men and horses in a sprawling mass.

Horsemen in the second rank tried to get their mounts to weave between or jump those who had gone down, but they then took a volley from the second rank, which halted most of them. Those that regrouped were dragged from their saddles and impaled on bayonets.

Further waves of cavalry attacks were launched, but Von Sporcken's men closed ranks, redressed and began to

advance once more. The finest cavalry in Europe was being ripped to shreds, and there was no hope of rallying them. The technique of the unsupported charge of cavalry en masse was being defeated by the defensive firepower of unsupported infantry in line.

VICTORY FOR MUSKET AND BAYONET
With the French cavalry in ruins and their center wide open, now was the time for the Allied cavalry to strike and pour through de Contades's line. But their general, Lord George Sackville, did not charge, and his conduct and that of the British and German cavalry was to become a scandal. Their behavior contrasted with the bravery of the French, who made yet two more cavalry charges, including one straight into the point-blank fire of a large Allied battery in the center.

Minden was unquestionably a battle won by the musket and the bayonet. The lesson for the cavalry was that if infantry stood and could deliver disciplined firepower at close range they could stop the gallop charge in its tracks.

TIMELINE

1500–1000BC	1000–500BC	500BC–0AD	0–500AD	500–1000AD	1000–1500AD	1500–2000AD

Siege of Quebec 1759

The Battle of Quebec was one of the shortest in history, lasting no longer than 15 minutes. It is ironic, then, that the generals on either side should succumb to mortal gunshot wounds during its brisk interplay of firefighting.

FRENCH AND INDIAN WAR

BRITISH VICTORY

KEY FACTS

WHO British army and navy under the control of General James Wolfe against Louis-Joseph, Marquis de Montcalm leading the French army.

WHAT The French ineffectively delivered their gunfire from too great a distance, while the English waited until they were within close range and dispensed their front line within two volleys.

WHERE Quebec, Canada.

WHEN September 13, 1759

WHY The British had made an amphibious assault on Quebec, the key possession among France's colonial territories in North America.

OUTCOME Both generals were fatally injured in the battle, but Quebec fell to the British, who would go on to capture the French colonies in North America.

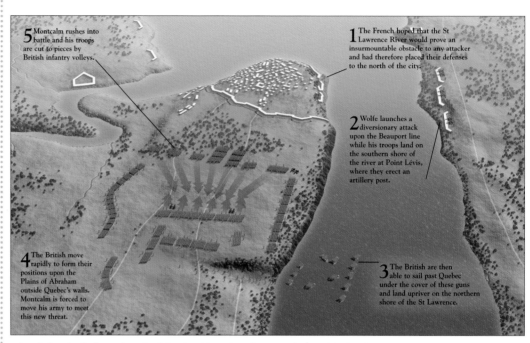

5 Montcalm rushes into battle and his troops are cut to pieces by British infantry volleys.

1 The French hoped that the St Lawrence River would prove an insurmountable obstacle to any attacker and had therefore placed their defenses to the north of the city.

2 Wolfe launches a diversionary attack upon the Beauport line while his troops land on the southern shore of the river at Point Lévis, where they erect an artillery post.

4 The British move rapidly to form their positions upon the Plains of Abraham outside Quebec's walls. Montcalm is forced to move his army to meet this new threat.

3 The British are then able to sail past Quebec under the cover of these guns and land upriver on the northern shore of the St Lawrence.

A lot of planning had gone into the defensive siting of Quebec, to make use of the local terrain. In the end, a fierce exchange of artillery fire would be enough to swiftly to decide the outcome in favor of the British attacking force.

LOCATION

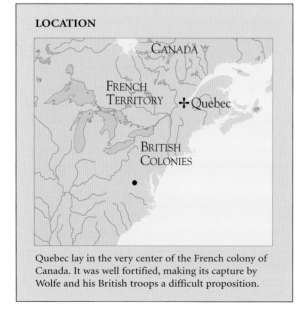

Quebec lay in the very center of the French colony of Canada. It was well fortified, making its capture by Wolfe and his British troops a difficult proposition.

Quebec was France's much-prized North American colonial capital. When it became plain that General Wolfe, after an amphibious mission along the St Lawrence River, had managed to slip his troops through a gap in the bankside defenses to muster above the city, General Montcalm, the French commander, mustered his men as quickly as he could. But Wolfe had caught him off guard, and was effectively able to give battle on the Plains of Abraham on his terms.

Montcalm next made the fatal error of committing his troops too early to battle, instead of taking up a more defensive posture. His men delivered their gunfire from so distant a range that it proved ineffective. By contrast, the English infantry waited until their enemies had advanced well within musket range, then delivered their volleys smartly to maximum effect. The French were swiftly cut to pieces, but both Wolfe and Montcalm died from mortal gunshot wounds received in the short battle. After the bloody battle, the British began erecting siege lines, but the city capitulated once its garrison had been defeated in the field.

TIMELINE

1500–1000BC	1000–500BC	500BC–0AD	0–500AD	500–1000AD	1000–1500AD	1500–2000AD

Quiberon Bay 1759

KEY FACTS

Who
The British navy under Admiral Sir Edward Hawke against Admiral Marquis de Conflans and the French navy.

What
An opportunist attack by Admiral Hawke, catching the French in shallow, rocky waters where they believed confrontation was unthinkable, reaped a handsome result for the British.

Where
Quiberon Bay, near St Nazaire, France.

When
November 20, 1759

Why
France planned an invasion of Scotland, but several British warships set out to interrupt the preparation of its fleet near Quiberon Bay.

Outcome
The defeat shattered the French navy and put an end to their plans to sail on Scotland.

The Seven Years' War (1756–1763) was not a profitable military venture for France, and at Quiberon Bay, in its own waters, its navy would experience one of its most humiliating defeats.

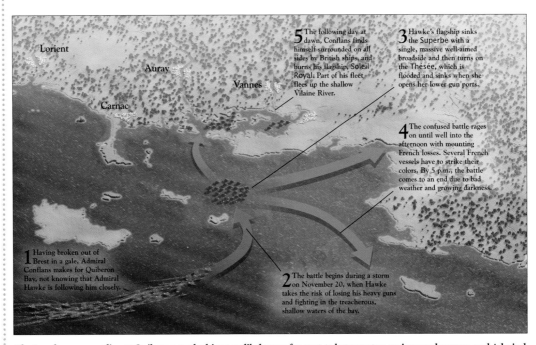

5 The following day at dawn, Conflans finds himself surrounded on all sides by British ships, and burns his flagship, Soleil Royal. Part of his fleet flees up the shallow Vilaine River.

3 Hawke's flagship sinks the Superbe with a single, massive well-aimed broadside and then turns on the Thésée, which is flooded and sinks when she opens her lower gun ports.

4 The confused battle rages on until well into the afternoon with mounting French losses. Several French vessels have to strike their colors. By 5 p.m., the battle comes to an end due to bad weather and growing darkness.

1 Having broken out of Brest in a gale, Admiral Conflans makes for Quiberon Bay, not knowing that Admiral Hawke is following him closely.

2 The battle begins during a storm on November 20, when Hawke takes the risk of losing his heavy guns and fighting in the treacherous, shallow waters of the bay.

The treacherous coastline at Quiberon made this an unlikely spot for a set-to between two major naval powers, and Admiral Hawke verged on the reckless in his pursuit of the French into these waters.

LOCATION

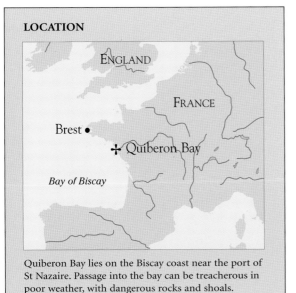

Quiberon Bay lies on the Biscay coast near the port of St Nazaire. Passage into the bay can be treacherous in poor weather, with dangerous rocks and shoals.

Quiberon Bay is a shallow, rocky and dangerous stretch of water and a far from ideal spot for a sea battle. But having shadowed the French to the bay where their commander Admiral Marquis de Conflans hoped to find sanctuary, Admiral Hawke overlooked the obvious dangers, made far worse by a oncoming gale, to signal his captains to "Go at them!" The French were shocked that their enemy would be so bold as to fight them inside the bay during a gale, and shock turned to panic when Hawke's flagship sunk the *Superbe* with a single broadside. The *Thésée* sunk like a stone in the foaming waves when her captain ordered the lower gun ports opened to fire back at the British with her heaviest guns, allowing water to flood the ship.

VICTORY IN ADVERSITY

The battle raged on with intense ferocity for another three hours, but a critical British naval success had been achieved in potentially treacherous waters. The French plans to sail to attack Scotland were in ruins, and its defeat at Quiberon Bay was described as its "Trafalgar" of the Seven Years' War—which it would ultimately lose.

TIMELINE

1500–1000BC	1000–500BC	500BC–0AD	0–500AD	500–1000AD	1000–1500AD	1500–2000AD

Quiberon Bay

QUIBERON BAY

Admiral Sir Edward Hawke does not have the familiar ring of Admiral Horatio Nelson, perhaps, but he must be chalked up as another in a long line of able British sea commanders. At Quiberon Bay he conducted what to the French seemed an unthinkable, highly risky attack on their navy in shallow, rocky waters off the coast near St Nazaire. Hawke's opportunist success was later recalled as the French "Trafalgar" of the Seven Years' War. It was undoubtedly a real-life instance of "He who dares, wins."

Siege of Havana 1762

When the Earl of Albermarle laid painstaking siege to the fortress of Morro, an outpost of Spanish-held Havana, many feared he was wasting precious time, with his men succumbing to yellow fever, and the hurricane season approaching. Could his patient approach pay off?

KEY FACTS

WHO	An amphibious British force led by the Earl of Albermarle, against combined Spanish forces led by Juna de Prado, the commander in chief, and Admiral Gutierre de Hevia.
WHAT	The Earl of Albermarle decided that taking the fortress of Morro, at the entrance to Havana harbor, was the key to taking the city itself. But at one point it looked like he had run out of time.
WHERE	Havana, Cuba.
WHEN	June 6–August 14, 1762
WHY	The British were involved in a colonial war with Spain in the Americas, and Havana was an important Caribbean base for the Spanish fleet.
OUTCOME	Havana would actually be returned to Spain as part of the treaty signed at the end of the Seven Years' War, but its loss in 1762 was a serious blow to its naval power status.

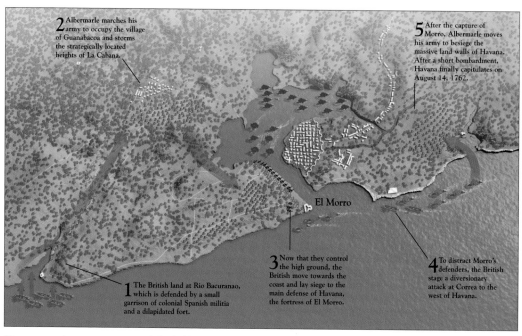

2 Albermarle marches his army to occupy the village of Guanabacoa and storms the strategically located heights of La Cabana.

5 After the capture of Morro, Albermarle moves his army to besiege the massive land walls of Havana. After a short bombardment, Havana finally capitulates on August 14, 1762.

El Morro

3 Now that they control the high ground, the British move towards the coast and lay siege to the main defense of Havana, the fortress of El Morro.

4 To distract Morro's defenders, the British stage a diversionary attack at Correa to the west of Havana.

1 The British land at Rio Bacuranao, which is defended by a small garrison of colonial Spanish militia and a dilapidated fort.

Havana, as an important port, was defended by several fortifications. When the British appeared to spend most time on reducing a single fort guarding the harbor entrance, there were fears they were wasting precious resources.

Moving to wrest the vital port of Havana from Spanish control during the Seven Years' War, the British caught their colonial rivals off guard by landing at the mouth of the Bacuranao river and moving swiftly to occupy the strategic heights of La Cabana and the village of Guanabacoa. La Cabana gave the British a commanding position above the Bay of Havana, where they could position artillery before moving to take control of the fortress of Morro, which defended the entrance to Havana's harbor. Albermarle, the British commander, was criticized for his slow but methodical strategy, and it's possible he underestimated the extent of the Morro fortifications. The Morro and its Spanish defenders were able to hold out for many days, costing the British dearly in numbers of men lost to yellow fever in the sticky tropical climate.

However, when it finally fell, it meant that Albermarle could march with his men smartly around the south of the Bay and lay siege to the city itself, which eventually capitulated on August 14, 1762. The siege was over and Britain had won a great victory over her colonial rivals.

LOCATION

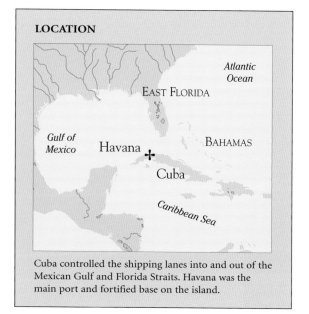

Atlantic Ocean

EAST FLORIDA

Gulf of Mexico

Havana

BAHAMAS

Cuba

Caribbean Sea

Cuba controlled the shipping lanes into and out of the Mexican Gulf and Florida Straits. Havana was the main port and fortified base on the island.

TIMELINE

1500–1000BC	1000–500BC	500BC–0AD	0–500AD	500–1000AD	1000–1500AD	1500–2000AD

Maymyo 1767

When the might of the Chinese army rolled into Burma at the start of the Sino-Burmese War, victory appeared certain for the larger army. But the Burmese terrain, with its jungles and mountains, is ideal for a plucky, and smart, local soldier with the know-how to exploit the situation.

KEY FACTS

WHO Maha Thiha Thura, commander of the Burmese military forces, against the Chinese army led by General Mingrui.

WHAT The Burmese encircled a retreating Chinese army and effectively massacred them, with General Mingrui committing suicide.

WHERE Maymyo, modern-day Pyinoolwin, Burma.

WHEN 1767

WHY The Chinese had invaded Burma and Maha Thiha Thura used his heavily outnumbered infantry in guerrilla warfare tactics.

OUTCOME Sickened by defeat, yet undeterred, the Chinese would launch a further invasion, but once again Maha Thiha Thura would be in the thick of the action to repel them.

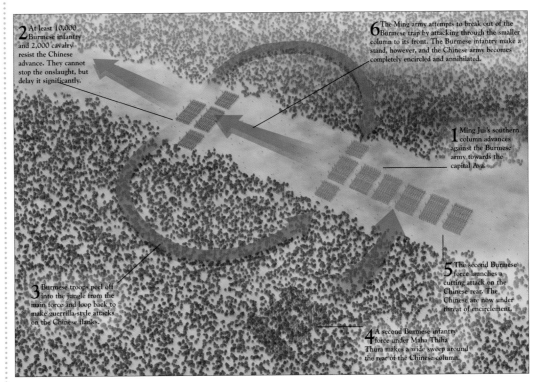

2 At least 10,000 Burmese infantry and 2,000 cavalry resist the Chinese advance. They cannot stop the onslaught, but delay it significantly.

6 The Ming army attempts to break out of the Burmese trap by attacking through the smaller column to its front. The Burmese infantry make a stand, however, and the Chinese army becomes completely encircled and annihilated.

1 Ming Jui's southern column advances against the Burmese army towards the capital Ava.

3 Burmese troops peel off into the jungle from the main force and loop back to make guerrilla-style attacks on the Chinese flanks.

5 The second Burmese force launches a cutting attack on the Chinese rear. The Chinese are now under threat of encirclement.

4 A second Burmese infantry force under Maha Thiha Thura makes a wide sweep around the rear of the Chinese column.

The massive Ming army must have presented an impressive sight as it rolled forwards, but the outnumbered Burmese were not intimidated. Jungle terrain such as this was custom-ordered for their guerrilla-style tactics.

LOCATION

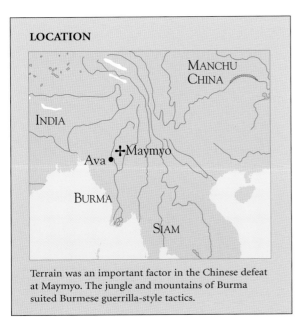

Terrain was an important factor in the Chinese defeat at Maymyo. The jungle and mountains of Burma suited Burmese guerrilla-style tactics.

When Miha Thiha Thura caught up with the Chinese army at Maymyo, they were already ailing from tropical diseases, starvation and extreme fatigue as their strategy for taking Burma unravelled. A pincer action against the Burmese capital of Ava failed after one force became isolated and cut off by the Burmese infantry who, naturally enough, had the major advantage of being more familiar with their country's convoluted terrain.

They put up such an impressive defense at Kaughton, a fortified position, that the northern arm of the Chinese pincer was stopped dead in its tracks, and then put into retreat. The Chinese infantry of the southern column, therefore, were left isolated against the increasing Burmese guerrilla-style attacks. Then, as a killer blow, the entire army was encircled by Miha Thiha Thura's men. The Chinese suffered large casualties from Burmese archers and gunners as they moved in for the kill, and General Mingrui, electing not to flee the field, instead committed suicide.

TIMELINE

1500–1000BC	1000–500BC	500BC–0AD	0–500AD	500–1000AD	1000–1500AD	1500–2000AD

Glossary

artillery Projectile or ranged weapons, such as bows, slings, and catapults, for discharging missiles.

flank The right and left sides of a formation in an army, often vulnerable to attack. The term is also a verb in this meaning, to "flank" someone or something.

Frederick the Great Also Frederick the II, the King of Prussia, particularly known for the spread of Enlightenment in Prussia and his victories in the Seven Years' War.

matchlock A slow-burning match over a hole in the breech of a musket that ignited its firing charge.

musket A smooth-bored, long-barreled, muzzleloading gun carried by an infantryman, fired from the shoulder, in part, due to its weight.

Prussia The former controlling state of the German Empire, ceasing in 1947 with the creation of Germany and, eventually, becoming a vast region of Russia.

samurai The warriors of feudal Japan who acted as servants of Daimyos and lords of their lands.

Seven Years' War A war from 1754 to 1763 involving every major European power except the Ottoman Empire that would split Europe into two coalitions and affect the future of the Americas as well.

tuo cheng A herd of camels tied together to form an unconventional wall during a battle between the Zhungarians and the Chinese.

versos A nickname, meaning "murderers," for the light artillery pieces on swivels used by Austria to combat the Turks' archers.

Further Reading

Baldanza, Katherine. *Ming China and Vietnam: Negotiating Borders in Early Modern Asia*. Cambridge, UK. Cambridge University Press, 2016.

Blanning, Tim. *Frederick the Great: King of Prussia*. New York, NY: Random House-Penguin, 2016.

Dennis, Peter. *Wargame: The English Civil Wars 1642–1651*. Solihull, West Midlands, UK:. Helion and Company Limited, 2016.

Kim, JaHyun. A *Korean War Captive in Japan, 1597–1600. The Writings of Kang Hang*. New York, NY: Columbia University Press, 2013.

McCabe, Richard. *"Ungaineful Arte": Poetry, Patronage, and Print in the Early Modern Era*. New York, NY: Oxford University Press, 2016.

Rawski, Evelyn S. *Early Modern China and Northeast Asia: Cross-Border Perspectives*. Cambridge, UK: Cambridge University Press, 2015.

Te Brake, Wayne P. *Religious War and Religious Peace in Early Modern Europe*. Cambridge, UK: Cambridge University Press, 2017.

Vaporis, Constantine Namikos. *Voices of Early Modern Japan: Contemporary Accounts of Daily Life During the Age of the Shoguns*. Boulder, CO: Westview Press, 2013.

Varlik, Nükhet. *Plague and Empire in the Early Modern Mediterranean World: The Ottoman Experience, 1347–1600*. New York, NY: Cambridge University Press, 2015.

Whitman, Jon. *Romance and History: Imagining Time from the Medieval to the Early Modern Period*. Cambridge, UK: Cambridge University Press, 2015.

Index